How to be a Soul Physician

Learning How Christ Meets the Deepest Longings of a Soul through the Grace of Prayer

Bill Thrasher

Published by:

Berea Publishing Co.

Camino a Berea #70
Localidad Los Fresnos
Charo, Michoacán 61311
Mexico
(443) 333-1631
www.bereapublishing.com

To purchase Dr. Thrasher's books in English and Spanish
please go to **www.victoriouspraying.com**

Contents

FOREWARD

My first class at Moody Graduate School was a one-week modular course taught by Dr. Bill Thrasher. At the end of those five days I left saying, "The next class I take will be whatever that man teaches." So a few months later I was sitting in his classroom again for a course on prayer, and again God impacted my spiritual life in immeasurable ways. Almost fifteen years later I have been able to sit through Dr. Thrasher's prayer class five times, and I can tell you the insights and principles never get old. As he says, "You can never overemphasize the resting truth of God's loving acceptance." (p. 40) In fact, that truth takes on fresh meaning with each new season of life.

It is hard to imagine Dr. Thrasher as someone who wrestles with acceptance by God and fear of man. But that is exactly the point. Dr. Thrasher is the only kind of person who exists—one who struggles with identity issues. He does seem unique, however, because of his deliberate commitment to address these struggles with God's truth over many years. Dr. Thrasher has spent his adult life, not doing an experiment, but being the experiment. Over and over again he has admitted his inner weakness, addressed that weakness with God's precious promises, and persevered with confidence in God. Because of his discipline to keep records of God's faithful work and his willingness to share what he has learned through teaching and writing, we can all be beneficiaries of his lifelong quest to know the deepest longings of his soul met in Christ.

Just reading or hearing testimony of the illumination God has given Dr. Thrasher will not automatically mean the same for us. We have to sincerely mimic the deliberate pursuit of God's truth and God's touch that he has modeled. We have to believe, as he says, that the truth of God's gracious acceptance in Christ "is not just nice; it is utterly necessary." (p. 39) May the Holy Spirit open the eyes of your spiritual understanding as you read the following pages which are saturated with scriptural treasure that can change your thinking and as a result transform your life.

One of our richest treasures in Christ is peace. Jesus is our peace so we can be in a right relationship with God, and the Holy Spirit produces the fruit of peace as we walk each day looking to God in faith. The Bible says God's peace will stand like a strong guard over our minds and hearts. In fact, it says this peace will be so powerful in our lives that we will not even be able to find words to describe it. May Dr. Thrasher's testimony and instruction be God's instruments directing you to experience the reality of that deep peace in your soul just as they have been in mine.

When Dr. Thrasher comes to teach at our church, I tell people I cannot think of any gift I would rather give than for them to be able to sit under his instruction on prayer and spiritual rest. I feel the same for anyone about to open the pages of this book. You are holding a prize that can enable you to experience the reality of God's fresh and freeing work. If you read this book without feeling that wave of relief, read it again.

Ross Robinson

Second Forward

One day, in the spring of 1983 at the Moody Bible Institute, I knelt **once again** beside my bed on the 9th floor of Culberson Hall, and **again**, confessed my sins. Guilt-ridden and miserable, I paused, and in a moment of total honesty asked, "Lord, if this is the Christian life, why would I ever want to share it with others."

The answer to this question was the most crucial of my life. As a student in the Evangelism Major at Moody, I was ready to throw in the towel. I noticed that the following chapel sessions were going to deal with the theme of "guilt". I knew from experience that these teachings would only cause me to feel guilty for feeling guilty. I longed to skip chapel. But that too, would result in increased guilt.

So I attended the chapels. It was the final session that God used to transform my life. The speaker was unknown to me. He began with a very simple question: "If Jesus said, 'Come unto Me, all ye who labor and are heavy laden, and I will give you rest for your souls", why do most Christians I know carry an incredible burden of guilt?" I quickly sat forward in my chair in the balcony of Torrey Gray

Auditorium. My heart cried out, longing for the answer to that question.

The chapel speaker that day was Dr. William Thrasher. My tears of joy and relief freely flowed as he expounded the truths of Romans 8:1: "There is therefore now no condemnation for those who are in Christ Jesus."

After this, I took every class I could from Dr. Thrasher and was richly blessed in each one, as he so simply but effectively helped the students to see the truths concerning God's acceptance and love of His children.

For the past few years, my wife and I have had the immense privilege of having Dr. Thrasher and his family participate in our summer youth camps where the Lord has allowed us to serve Him in the mountains of Central Mexico. Here, his spiritual life teachings now bless our Mexican believers, our fellow missionaries, our children and again, our own lives, as they did those many years ago at the Moody Bible Institute.

My prayer is that God will use Dr. Thrasher to free you from your load of guilt and that the truths in this book will become a reality and blessing in your life.

Ted Clark

Dedication

It brings me great pleasure to dedicate this book to the Lord and special recognition of His gracious work in the lives of my students these past thirty years. Paul spoke of ministry as a two-way street—"That is, that I may be encouraged together with you while among you, each of us by the other's faith, both yours and mine" (Romans 1:12). In countless ways I have been encouraged and supported by the lives of my students as I have seen them look to God and be His special instruments around the world.

I wish it were possible to highlight every one of them by name, but I have chosen two as representatives of countless others. Ross Robinson is a graduate of one of our MA programs. Ted Clark went through our undergraduate program at Moody. I sit back and marvel at the work God has done in and through each of these two men.

The Old Testament priests were to retire at age fifty (I'm glad I live in this era!). However, they were not to quit ministering but rather to "assist others in their work" (Numbers 8:26). I have sought to keep this principle in mind as I minister at this phase of life. It has been an enormous privilege to minister alongside both of these fine men and their families—one here in the States and the other in numerous trips to Mexico. In both cases, whether it is in the local church in Greenville, S.C., or on the mission field in Mexico, I have wept with gratitude to see these students doing exploits far beyond what I could have ever done.

It is very fitting to praise God for His grace in their lives, families, and ministry. I invite you to pray for them and the thousands of others they represent.

INTRODUCTION

May God greatly bless you as you read this book. There is no greater joy or privilege than to be "God's fellow worker" (I Cor. 3:9). It is worth your "labor" to do everything you can to present yourself and others as "complete in Christ" (Col. 1:28-29).

Rembrandt is recognized by many people as one of the most famous painters who ever lived. Growing up in the seventeenth century in the Netherlands, he produced over two thousand paintings, etchings, and drawings. If you were to buy any of these paintings today, you would pay an enormous price. You might wonder why he had to declare bankruptcy in his later years since he was recognized, even in his early years, as a great artist. The reason is that the value of his work was not determined until quite a bit later. It was when very large sums of money began to be offered for his paintings that their worth was established.

God, in His infinite wisdom, fashioned your life (Ps. 139:13-16). However, it is the great price that He offered for your redemption that reveals your great worth in His eyes. God gave His Son as the payment for your salvation:

> Knowing that you were not redeemed with
> perishable things like silver or gold from your
> futile way of life inherited from your
> forefathers, but with precious blood, as of a
> lamb unblemished and spotless, the blood of
> Christ. (I Pet. 1:18-19)

The truths of this book are very precious to me. If you were to offer millions of dollars in exchange for the experience of Christ's acceptance (Section 1), authority (Section 2), motivation and enablement (Section 3), and continual cleansing (Section 5), I would not be even tempted to entertain the offer. The study guide at the back of the book is designed to help you digest and treasure these truths so that you will speak of them as "precious and magnificent" (2 Peter 1:4).

God graciously offers His loving aid in everyone's battle with anger (Section 4), guilt (Section 5), and fear (Section 6). You can be "more than a conqueror" in these battles and experience the wonderful gift that Jesus called "rest for your soul" (Section 7).

Over one hundred years ago, D. L. Moody urged the church to return to the training of "soul physicians." These are men and women who have learned to lean upon the Holy Spirit in both diagnosing the condition of the soul and in aiding others to experience the blessing that can be found in the Lord Jesus Christ. True ministry flows from the inward person (John 7:37-39) and genuine growth involves a strengthening of our spirits (Luke 1:80; Eph. 3:16). This book is designed to allow God to do a work in you that He may freely work through you. It is aimed at equipping you to meet the spiritual needs of others and to shepherd, exhort, and guide God's people. Training people to be soul physicians involves obeying Paul's instruction to Timothy to first "pay close attention to yourself and your teaching," which results not only in one's own sanctification, but also in becoming a living epistle and overflowing to others in fulfilling the Great Commission. I have written this book to enable you to abound in the work of the Lord as you experience the grace of prayer. As God liberates and frees you, you will also be equipped to overflow and aid others by pointing them to Christ—the only One who can meet the deepest longings of a soul.

Prayer is the means that will enable you to receive Christ's gifts and to sustain you in your work as a soul physician. Do you understand that God not only saves you by grace but also wants to teach you to live and pray in His grace? Or could your Christian experience be characterized by the truth of Galatians 3:3?

> Are you so foolish? Having begun by the Spirit,
> are you now being perfected by the flesh?

Let us pray together in faith that God will illuminate our minds and hearts to understand and experience the grace of prayer and thus enter into what Jesus called rest for our souls in the midst of the demands of life and in all of the circumstances that we encounter in our work as soul physicians.

SECTION ONE

NEED FOR ACCEPTANCE— EXPERIENCING THE GRACE OF GOD'S DELIGHT IN YOU

The root of every unhealthy addiction is in some way related to a lack of understanding the truth of God's love and delight. To be sure, some addictions such as workaholism can be applauded by society. However, if we are working to try to hear the message that God spoke to His Son—"Thou art my beloved Son in whom I am well pleased"—we are working for the wrong reason.

God loves His children with the same intensity that He loves His own Son (see John 17:23). As you read this section, open your heart to let God first speak this message to you that He can effectively speak it through you. As a soul physician you will be aiding others to believe and experience their theology which speaks of God's delight in them. You will also aid them in learning how to detect the lies they are believing in order to be set free from the fear of man and to be understood and loved by a perfect Father—the most reconcilable person with whom they will ever have a relationship. Believe God to enlighten the eyes of your heart as you read this section.

CHAPTER ONE

OVERCOMING THE BARRIER *"I KNOW THAT"* AND EXPERIENCING SPONTANEOUS PRAISE

I was studying and teaching the book of Galatians over a period of years when God began to give me an understanding of this concept of "resting truths" that enabled me to grasp what it practically means to live under the grace of God. I found myself asking God, "I know and believe these truths, but how can I know if I'm truly resting in them?" The first insight I learned was that if there are not times of spontaneous praise for God's love and acceptance, then I am not resting in this truth.

The Bible is full of spontaneous praise. Psalm 139:17-18 is one example, "How precious also are Thy thoughts to me, O God! How vast is the sum of them! If I should count them, they would outnumber the sand. When I awake, I am still with Thee." David praises God because He has him on His mind day and night. If you have someone continually on your mind, that person is very important to you. There may have been times that you would like to have put yourself on someone else's mind. In fact, the girl who became my wife was on my mind continually before I was ever on her mind—quite a bit before. I carried her on my mind because I delighted in her. I still carry her on my mind. In a far more perfect way God keeps His children continually in His thoughts.

You and I need somebody who is "wild" about us. That is how God created the human heart. Only He can think of us day and night and give us His full attention. In fact, in His infinite love He can focus on you as if you were the only person in the world, without neglecting any other business that He is doing in caring for the entire universe.

I remember expressing the truth of justification by faith to a group of college students. They wrote down all that I said and one freshman female student looked up at me as if to say, "Give me the next point." I thought to myself, "Wait a minute; what have I just said?" I had just stated that because of Christ's death on the cross, God looks at us not only as if we have never sinned but also as if we have always perfectly obeyed Him. He has declared us righteous in His sight and perfectly, completely, and absolutely loves and accepts us as His children.

What if I had known that this freshman girl had her thoughts on a certain young man in that class? What if I had gone up to her before class and said, "I realize that your mind is continually on Ben and what I also know is that Ben is continually thinking about you. In fact, he absolutely adores you—just as you are. He so delights in you that he

thinks everything about you is great." What do you think
her response would be? Would it be, "Oh, that is nice, give
me your next point." No! The desire to delight in this truth
and meditate upon it would be as natural as breathing. And
there would not necessarily be anything wrong with this
response. It is sad when we treat the truth of God as if it
were unreal and secondary. It should rather be the very
truth that defines our very lives. You, like the apostle John,
should view yourself as the disciple whom Jesus loved
(John 21:20). He did not view himself as the only one he
loved, for he clearly taught God loved the world. However,
he personalized this truth in the same way that Apostle
Paul did when he wrote Galatians 2:20:

> I have been crucified with Christ; and it is no
> longer I who live, but Christ lives in me; and the
> life which I now live in the flesh I live by faith in
> the Son of God, **who loved me** and gave
> Himself up for me. (Galatians 2:20, emphasis
> added)

It is the personalization of this truth that evokes
spontaneous praise in your heart to God when you sense
God's personal delight in you.

Perhaps it is for this reason that Dr. Lewis Sperry Chafer,
after teaching theology for most of his life and writing
volumes of Systematic Theology, spontaneously exclaimed
one day to his students, "Men, I think I'm just about to
understand what it means to be justified by faith!" When
one grasps this truth to the extent that he senses the favor

and pleasure of a God who rejoices over His people like a bridegroom rejoices over his bride, praise is the natural response.

It is what author S.J. Hill spoke of when he wrote: [1]

> The blemishes, scars, and extra pounds may weigh on your heart, but they don't weigh on His. God loves your freckles. He loves your funky-shaped toes. He loves you—just as you are. He loves your uniqueness. He loves the smile that only *your* face can radiate. He loves you when you're awake, vibrant, and full of life. And He loves you when you're down, struggling, and lethargic.
>
> He even loves you when you're sleeping. He gets excited when you wake up—even with the morning breath and "sleep" tucked in the corners of your eyes. He can't wait to hear your voice. He looks forward to your first thoughts. He loves accompanying you throughout the day. He enjoys being with you at work. He isn't watching the clock or tapping His toe until five o'clock. Just being with you is enough. He loves talking with you, traveling with you, and being tender with you. He loves watching you enjoy His creation. He smiles when you look at the mountains, sea, or sky and think of Him.

---

[1] S.J. Hill, *Enjoying God* (Lake Mary, Florida: Relevant Books, 2001), 3.

> The truth is, God really likes you. In fact, He
> enjoys you. You may not think you measure
> up to supermodel or Mr. GQ status, but He
> does. Thanks to the gracious act of His Son,
> He sees you perfectly redeemed.

He has not only spoken about His love, but He has
demonstrated it to you when you were hostile against Him
(Rom. 5:6-10). Ravi Zacharias makes the following
observation about how many of us approach the subject of
God's love when he writes these words:

> The idea that God loves us can easily become
> merely a theoretical statement. We say it
> often enough, yet I am absolutely certain that
> even if this truth sinks home, the significance
> of it seems to wear off with time. We forget
> the immensity of the truth that God loves us
> just as we are, in the frailty and the struggle
> with which we live. Understanding this must
> more than inform the mind; it must stir the
> heart with emotion. That is the
> understanding that feeds wonder. When the
> truth remains abstract, the soul does not live
> off the treasure. [2]

Are you ready to cross over the barrier of "I know that" to
experiencing an epidemic of expressing spontaneous praise

---

[2] Ravi Zacharias, *Recapture the Wonder* (Brentwood, TN: Integrity
Publishers, 2003), 114.

for His love for you? Do you believe that He loves you? Are you willing to pray that God would overwhelm you with an awareness of His love? Are there other people in your life for whom you should also pray this same prayer?

CHAPTER TWO

EXPERIENCING GOD'S GRACIOUS DELIGHT IN YOU

Martin Lloyd-Jones was a medical doctor who sensed God's call to leave his medical practice to preach God's Word. He illustrated the believer's standing in grace through the analogy of a poor, pathetic beggar. Viewing a beautiful, glorious palace, the miserable man who lived on the streets saw the festive activities and bountiful provisions that those in the palace enjoyed day after day. Meanwhile, he shivered in the cold, clothed in rags and begging for food. One day the son of the king came to him, took him by the hand, and introduced him to his father, the king. Providing royal garments for him, he told him that he could enjoy permanent favor and access to the king, as if he were the king's son.

The Enjoyment of God's Loving Acceptance and Delight

Do you clearly see the gospel analogy? If you are a genuine believer in Christ, God loves you with the same intensity as His own Son (John 17:23—Look it up!). Do you see yourself as one who is loved by the King of kings and who has continual and permanent access to Him and His spiritual riches because of His Son? Or do you see yourself as the pathetic man on the street? You may live physically on the street, but if you know Jesus you can enjoy the King's palace. You may have millions of dollars in this world, but if you do not acknowledge Jesus you are living in great poverty.

Are many people outside the church today because we who are Christians represent the Christian life so poorly? Are we living as spiritual paupers when we were meant to live as children of the heavenly King? God is not pleased if you do not agree with this truth. Such a decision would not be a sign of humility, but rather of rebellion. The Christian is to be a humble person, but humility is submitting to God and agreeing with Him. He said that because of the precious Lord Jesus' perfect life and cruel death, a follower of Jesus can enjoy peace with God and a permanent standing in His favor!

A former student of mine struggled to say the words, "God loves me." Such a statement according to her perception was prideful because she sensed it meant that she deserved His love. We do not deserve it, but His Son paid the price for our sins so that we can enjoy it. The precious words that describe the accomplishments of Jesus' death are not idle words.

How would you feel if as you were reading this book someone tapped you on your shoulder and asked to sit down next to you? You would respond, "It would depend on who the person is." Suppose it was a person who knew everything that you have ever done, everything you have ever said, and everything you have ever thought! How would you feel? Would you feel like running? What if I also told you that wherever you go he is always there. My dear friend, there is Someone with you at this moment who does know everything about you. He is the one Who offers you His amazing love and delight through His precious Son.

The Scriptures teach that Jesus has earned for us the "delight of God." Are you trying to earn it by your appearance? "If only I looked a certain way, then I would be a delightful person." Or are you trying to gain it through your performance, accomplishments, or status? The Psalmist speaks not only of our responsibility to delight in the Lord:

> <u>Delight</u> yourself in the LORD;
> And He will give you the desires of your heart. (Ps. 37:4, emphasis added)

but also of His delight in us!

> He brought me forth also into a broad place;
> He rescued me, because He <u>delighted</u> in me. (Ps. 18:19, emphasis added)

His delight in us is a gift that Jesus shed His blood to give us. This is the experience of God's grace. In fact, our delight in Him is merely a response to His delight in us just as "we love, because He first loved us" (I John 4:19).

Do you fear failure? In Christ you can receive complete justification:

> Therefore, having been <u>justified</u> by faith, we have peace with God through our Lord Jesus Christ. (Romans 5:1, emphasis added)

Do you fear rejection? In Christ you can experience God's reconciliation:

> For if, when we were God's enemies, we were reconciled to Him through the death of his Son, much more, having been <u>reconciled</u>, we shall be saved by his life. (Romans 5:10, emphasis added)

Do you fear God's wrath? In Christ you can experience Christ's propitiation, which simply means that God is satisfied with Christ's payment for sin and is righteously free to deliver you from His wrath and allow you to experience His kindness:

> Whom God displayed publicly as a propitiation in His blood through faith. This was to demonstrate His righteousness, because in the forbearance of God He passed over the sins previously committed. (Rom. 3:25)

The story that Floyd McClung relates provides a fitting conclusion to this chapter:

> During the Korean War, a pastor in a small rural village awoke one morning to find that his young son, his only child, had been killed. Apparently some soldiers had slipped in during the night and randomly executed a number of villagers in a brutal act of terrorism.

> The pastor was beside himself with grief. He had looked forward to his son someday following in his footsteps and becoming a pastor. Now his friends feared for his emotional stability, so severe was the grief he experienced over the boy's senseless death. It seemed so cruel, so unjust. His son was not in the army; he posed no threat to anyone. Why should he have been singled out like this?

> Finally the Korean pastor decided what he must do in return for this act of violence. He announced that he would hunt down the men who had killed his son and would not give up until he had found them. No obstacle would stand in his way, no hardship would deter him. This grief-stricken father resolved to do whatever it took.

> Amazingly, he was able to learn the identities of the two terrorists, slip behind enemy lines, and find out

where they lived. Early one morning he stole into their house and confronted them. The pastor told them who he was and that he knew they had murdered his son. "You owe me a debt," he said to them. "I have come to collect it."

The two men were obviously expecting to be killed in retaliation. But the pastor's next words astonished them. "You have taken my son," he said, "and now I want you to become my sons in his place."

The pastor stayed with them for several days, until he was able to persuade them to come with him. In time he adopted them as his legal sons. He loved them and cared for them. They became Christians, went to seminary, and were ordained. Today, these two men are pastors in Korea—all because of a father who was willing to do whatever it took to win them, whose love was utterly unstoppable.[3]

Do you come to God as a child of the King? Do you come to Him as the One who has freed you from His wrath, justified you, reconciled you, and who delights in you? In prayer, would you be willing to give your life to the Lord and allow Him to show to the world the realities of these truths?

---

[3] Floyd McClung, *Finding Friendship With God* (Ann Arbor, Mich.: Servant Publications, 1992), 149-150.

CHAPTER THREE

EXPERIENCING THE JOY OF BEING FATHERED AS YOU PRAY

Mark Ashton-Smith, a thirty-three year old lecturer at Cambridge University, capsized in some treacherous water while he was kayaking off the Isle of Wight in England. As he clung to his craft, he reached for his cell phone to call his father. Even though his father was 3,500 miles away training British troops in Dubai, his first instinct was to call his dad. At once his father relayed his son's call for help to the Coast Guard who had an installation less than a mile from his son's accident. Within twelve minutes a helicopter rescued Ashton-Smith.

When you are in serious danger, is your first impulse to call upon your heavenly Father? The answer to that question depends upon your perception of His character. Dr. Paul Vitz is a professor of psychology at New York University. He has written a book, *Faith of the Fatherless,* to describe his theory of the "defective father hypothesis." He believes that the atheist has a deep psychological need to reject God because of their bad relationship with their earthly father. Their disappointment in the rejection of their own father unconsciously justifies their rejection of God. He cites numerous examples such as Madelyn Murray O'Hair, the woman responsible for getting the Supreme Court to ban public school prayer in the 1960's. She hated her father and once attempted to kill him with a butcher knife. The French Philosopher Voltaire, a powerful critic of Christianity, hated his abusive father so much that he changed his family name from Arouet to Voltaire. Joseph Stalin was repeatedly beaten by his father. Such was also the experience of Adolph Hitler, whose father had been described as authoritative, selfish, and hard.

When Jesus' disciples came to Him and made their request to teach them to pray, our Lord's first words were, "When you pray say: 'Father'..." (Luke 11:1, 2) Your view of God will color your experience of prayer and the Christian life.

The entire Christian life begins with the experience of coming to know God as our Father. Listen to Galatians 4:5-7:

> So that He might redeem those who were under the law that we might receive the adoption as sons. Because you are sons, God has sent forth the Spirit of His son into our hearts, crying, "Abba! Father!" Therefore you are no longer a slave, but a son; and if a son, then an heir through God.

"Abba" is an Aramaic word that speaks of a very endearing and intimate relationship between a child and his father. It is found on the lips of Jesus when He is talking to His Father in Gethsemane (Mark 14:36), and it is also the relationship into which the Spirit of God seeks to lead every believer (Rom. 8:15). Jesus links the experience of prayer to knowing God as our Father:

> Now suppose one of you fathers is asked by his son for a fish; he will not give him a snake instead of a fish, will he? Or if he is asked for an egg, he will not give him a scorpion, will he? If you then, being evil, know how to give good gifts to your children, how much more will your heavenly Father give the Holy Spirit to those who ask him? (Luke 11:11-13)

If we project the imperfection of our earthly father onto God, we will reach some wrong conclusions. I remember reading the testimony of a woman who was raised by an alcoholic father and a mother who could inexplicably erupt in anger like a dormant volcano. She even found it difficult to sit through a sermon because of her feelings of condemnation and guilt. In her mind, God was not righteous, faithful, and true but unreliable, irrational, and unpredictable. She never knew when she would get hugged or slapped and could not figure out the reason for either one.

George MacDonald had a wonderful childhood and found great refuge in his loving father. However, he gave some profound advice for those who find no pleasure, warmth, and love in the name "father." In *The Heart of George MacDonald*, he states, "You must interpret the word by all that you have missed in life. All that human tenderness can give or devise in the nearness and readiness of love, all and infinitely more must be true of the perfect Father—of the maker of fatherhood."

All of us need to take seriously this advice, for there is only one Perfect Father—the Lord God. Go to Him to be healed from the hurts of your past. Let His truth uproot the lies so that you can view yourself as one for whom God gave His greatest sacrifice—His Son, in order to have an intimate relationship with you. When we begin to see Him for who He really is, our relationship with Him is what gives meaning to every aspect of our lives and it will enable us to begin to experience the grace of prayer and ministry.

Zach is one of my former students who grew up in what many would call tragic conditions as he was raised in the inner city project housing. God's grace found him and so transformed his life that one day a man approached and asked, "Who is your father?" The idea behind the question was, "If you are a chip off the block, I would sure like to meet the source." Zach replied, "I have never known my father, but Jesus is my daddy." Christ has truly fathered this young man who became not only the first in his family to graduate from high school but also from college and attend seminary. Today he is not only seeking to father his own children but has also founded a Christian school in the inner city of Chicago to help educate and father others.

My own dad never really knew his father, who died when my dad was only one year old. Because his mother was forced to go to work to provide for the family, he went to live with an aunt. When the aunt became pregnant with her own child, he was transferred to the home of the aunt's sister-in-law. It was here that he fell into the arms of his heavenly Father. Bernice Lewis ("B"), who had had several miscarriages, embraced him with great tenderness and love, enabling him to overcome the traumas of childhood and become a successful man. He would run home from the playground after hearing the taunts of the other children who said, "You have no Mama. You have no Daddy." When he arrived home, he would grab B's legs and say, "You are my mama, are you not?" She would affectionately respond, "Yes, I am your mama", and pointed him to the heavenly Father.

As a boy, I benefited from the heavenly Father's care of my dad. One day in his childhood, he saw a little red-headed girl and said to B, "Let's get one of those." She was a little hesitant, so my dad insisted that she tell Daddy Willie (her husband) to buy them one. She told him that it did not work that way and that he should pray about it. A few years later, he rode his bike twenty miles to the hospital to meet his new red-headed sister, Sylvia. God had given B a baby, and she was a wonderful sister to my father and later a wonderful aunt to me.

 C.S. Lewis, who influenced the Christian world with his writings, did not have an ideal father situation. His Welsh father, who was known for his fierce temper, sent him off to the British Empire at age 10 to attend a boarding school. Separated from his parents during these formative years, he was introduced to the love of his heavenly Father. He also developed a father/son relationship with a man who lived a century earlier, George MacDonald, who fathered him through his writings and the wisdom he had learned from his own father.

It is essential that each of us ponder our own pilgrimage with eyes of faith and the wisdom of God. As you respond correctly to the unique heritage God has given you-- whether tragic or blissful-- God will use this to open your eyes to the revelation of Himself--the one perfect Father. It is my prayer that God will use Section Four to help you ponder the trials of your heritage and that He will use the entire book to help you see the truth of our wonderful God who is the source of every blessing--including the gift of being fathered.[4] May God do such a profound work in you that countless others will also benefit as you do the work of a soul physician.

---

[4] For further insight on pondering your past, see Ken Canfield, *The Heart of a Father*. (Chicago, Moody Press 2006). For a look into the attributes of the heavenly Father, see my book *Living the Life God Has Planned* (Chicago, Moody Press 2001) p. 83-154.

CHAPTER FOUR

UPROOTING SATAN'S LIES ABOUT GOD AND MEETING THE PERFECT MATE

The story could be entitled, "The tale of two marriages." The first marriage was a nightmare. The husband put constant demands upon his wife. She lived under the burden of his continual expectations, which she could never meet. He gave her no help, aid, or encouragement to meet his demands—only a scolding and condemnation each time she failed. One day her husband died and the faithful wife grieved but also was relieved. Years later another man came and wooed her heart to become his wife. He was a very wealthy man and freely shared all his resources with her. She loved him freely, but her love was only a feeble response to his constant love for her. He lived by his solemn vow to continually love her, be faithful to her, never leave or forsake her, and enable her to be a fruitful and productive woman.

When one becomes a Christian, he is released from a marriage to law, through his participation in Christ's death and enters into a marriage relationship with Christ by participation in His resurrection. This is the clear teaching of Romans 7:1-6. However, in the mind of many believers are thoughts that reflect their old life. It was the German Reformer, Martin Luther, who said that many believers have enough religion to feel guilty about their sin but not enough to truly enjoy their new life in the Lord.

"Stronghold" is a term that is used to describe a thought pattern that gives Satan a protected place of influence. We need to trust God to uproot any lie that is not consistent with God's liberating truth that is revealed in the Bible. It is true that right living can only fully begin when there is right thinking. Furthermore, right thinking comes only when there is right thinking about God.

We may have to make the courageous choice to reject thoughts that we may have entertained for many years in order to receive the truth of the God who embraces us as His beloved whom He treasures. It is for this reason that He calls His people "His inheritance" (cf. Ps. 94:14, Eph. 1:18).[5] One who is treasured by God must see the wicked lies of such thoughts as, "I'm no good"; "I'll never amount to anything"; "No one could possibly love me." God in His grace has made it possible for Him to flood His hostile

---

[5] The believer in Christ not only has a rich inheritance because God is His Father, but also is termed "God's inheritance."

enemies (Rom. 5:10) with the reality of His reconciling love for them (Rom. 5:5).

The question of "Who art Thou, Lord?" (Acts 22:8), needs to be answered before the question, "What shall I do, Lord?" (Acts 22:10). Satan's most basic strategy is to distort man's understanding of God. You can clearly observe this strategy in Genesis 3:1-5, the first time we see Satan in operation against man. It is this wrong thinking that first led to man's rebellion against God. Because sin has perverted man's thinking, we must yield our lives and minds, in repentance and faith to Christ's love and His liberating truth rather than trying to merit God's love by performing for it.

It is hard to grasp the truth that the One who knows everything we have ever thought, said, or done would delight to have fellowship with us. The truth is that He loves us, not merely pities us. He delights in us as an artist does in his masterpiece. Sometimes an emotional interpretation of certain life experiences makes us feel less than cherished, loved and delightful. Our thoughts are, "I didn't get picked"; "I am unattractive,"; "I've been left on the shelf"; and "Nobody could ever love me". Test your thoughts by the following ...

What I feel or think about myself	What God says about me as a Christian according to Scripture
I am unworthy and un-acceptable	"I accept you." (Rom. 15:7)

What I feel or think about myself	What God says about me as a Christian according to Scripture
I am alone	"I'll live in you and you'll never have to be alone as I had to be when I died on the cross for you." (Gal. 2:20; Heb. 13:5-6)
I am not special to anyone or loved	"You are a precious person to me and I am continually thinking about you." (Ps. 139:17-18)
I do not have what it takes to be successful in life	"I'm continually devoted to you and will provide all your need to fulfill my purpose for you." (Rom. 8:31-32, 38-39)
I feel totally responsible for my life	"I've adopted you into my family and will take care of you, lead you, discipline you, and develop you as my child." (Gal. 4:5-6, Rom. 8:14)

What I feel or think about myself	What God says about me as a Christian according to Scripture
I feel despair as I think of the future	"I have a wonderful future for you that you will know joy and satisfaction for all eternity." (Rom. 8:18)
I fear Satan's power over my life	"I have defeated Satan and as you submit to my loving authority you can experience freedom." (James 4:7, I John 4:4)
I cannot overcome my sin habits	"I sent my Son to liberate you from sin's power and you are a winner and can now live in His strength." (Rom. 6:11-13)
I have no direction or plan for my life	"I have a unique plan of good works for you to accomplish." (Eph. 2:10)

What I feel or think about myself	What God says about me as a Christian according to Scripture
I am not qualified to fulfill God's plan as other people that I know	"My plan is unique for you because no one else has your exact physical features, upbringing, talents, and abilities, and even your unique weaknesses." (Ps. 139:13-16)
I don't think I can keep on going	"I'll continue to work in you because my glory is at stake." (Phil. 2:13; Ps. 22:3)
I am not attractive and fear failure	"I'll make you into a most attractive person in my eyes and allow you to fulfill my plan as you present your life to me." (Rom. 8:29; 12: 1-2)

Since we are under God's loving command to "have no other gods before Him" (Ex. 20:3), why not use this as a basis for a prayer of faith. Ask the Lord to uproot any ideas in your mind that are not true and worthy of Him. Believe Him to enable you to recognize these lies in a way that they can be rejected and replaced with His liberating truth. The following is a prayer that I have shared with thousands of people. While there is nothing magic about the words, each concept in the prayer is something for which we can all believe God:

> God, I want to know You above all else in life. I need the motivation, encouragement, and the wisdom to know how; but I desire it and want to desire it more. I believe You will overcome all obstacles and accomplish this in my life!

> For Your name's sake and for my eternal benefit, Amen.

Believe God for this and also trust Him to make you an instrument to encourage many others to believe God for this as well.

CHAPTER FIVE

EXPERIENCING A NEW LEVEL OF HONESTY AND INTIMACY WITH GOD

One day a student we will call Tom spontaneously shared with me a very profound lesson he had learned. As he was struggling with an ungodly habit, he related how he petitioned God to no avail for deliverance. One day a discerning man of God entered his life and in a gracious way asked him a question. "Why are you asking God to deliver you from this ungodly bondage? You do not really want Him to answer your prayer." Tom was completely devastated because this was the precise truth. He told me that one of the most humbling things that he ever did was to come to God and tell Him that he loved this ungodly habit and did not really want deliverance. You know what else he shared with me—that this was the beginning of the process of breaking the bondage to that ungodly habit!

It is this testimony that opened up Hebrews 4:15-16 to me:

> For we do not have a high priest who cannot
> sympathize with our weaknesses, but One who has
> been tempted in all things as we are, yet without sin.
> Therefore let us draw near with confidence to the
> throne of grace, so that we may receive mercy and find
> grace to help in time of need. (Heb. 4:15-16)

It was always amazing to **me** that God told me to draw near with confidence to **His** throne of grace. My problem was this—how do I do this when I am thinking the wrong thing and have the wrong attitude and I know I have the wrong attitude. The verb in this passage means to "come with freedom." This student "came with freedom" and "[drew] near with confidence" when he shared his heart with God. He experienced the promise of this verse. He received mercy and compassionate understanding in his weakness. He also found grace and new motivation and enablement to deal with his problem! God never honors deceit—even spiritual deceit.

Whom do you feel free to be totally transparent and honest with in your life? In 1994 two Americans responded to an invitation from the Russian Department of Education to teach biblical morals and ethics in the public schools, prisons, and businesses. On one occasion, they spoke to a large government-run orphanage. At this gathering, almost one hundred boys and girls who had been abandoned and abused were exposed to the message of Christ.

As the two missionaries shared, the orphans heard for the very first time the traditional story of Christ. As they spoke through their translators of Mary and Joseph's trip to Bethlehem and the birth of Jesus in the stable, both the children and the orphanage staff sat attentively on the edge of their seats and tried to grasp every word as they listened with amazement. Following the story each child was given pieces of cardboard to make a manger, paper cut from a yellow napkin to lay in the manger for straw, and a small piece of flannel cut from a worn-out nightgown to serve as a baby's blanket, and a doll-like baby. The orphans eagerly assembled their manger scene. As the missionaries walked around the room to see if anyone needed help, they noticed that six-year-old Misha had completely finished his project. All seemed well until one of the missionaries made the startling discovery of two babies in the manger. Quickly he called his translator in order to offer to tell the story again to Misha. Although Misha had heard the story only once, he repeated all the events of the story very accurately until he came to the part of Mary placing baby Jesus in the manger. Misha started to ad-lib and make up his own ending to the story. He said, "And when Maria laid the baby in the manger, Jesus looked at me and asked me if I had a place to stay. I told him I have no mamma and I have no papa, so I don't have any place to stay. Then Jesus told me I could stay with him. But I told him I couldn't, because I didn't have a gift to give him like everybody else did. But I wanted to stay with Jesus so much, so I thought about what I had that maybe I could use for a gift. I thought maybe if I kept him warm, that would be a good gift. So I asked Jesus, 'If I keep you warm, will that be a good enough gift?' And Jesus told me, 'If you keep me warm, that will be the best gift anybody ever gave me.' So I got into the manger, and then Jesus looked at me and he told me I could stay with him—for always."

Misha finished the story, his eyes overflowing with tears that splashed down his little cheeks. Placing his hands on his face he dropped his head to the table and he sobbed so hard that his shoulders shook. Misha had found Someone with whom he could be intimate—Someone who would never abandon him or abuse him. Someone who would stay with him ALWAYS! This is the One with whom you can afford to have a completely honest and intimate relationship! In the context of this loving intimacy, your soul and the souls of those to whom you minister can find encouragement and healing.

CHAPTER SIX

DELIGHT IN FEELING UNDERSTOOD AS YOU PRAY

The Christian church has greatly benefited from the life and ministry of Joni Erickson Tada. The life of this young, beautiful, and athletic girl was completely changed one day when she dove into a lake and struck a rock. Paralysis resulted from the accident and she is now a quadriplegic. Her witness has become worldwide through the movie of her life, her books, and her radio ministry, as well as her other compassionate outreaches.

It can be said that God wins His victories in the midst of apparent defeat. In her new condition, Joni felt so desperate that she even begged her friends to give her some pills so she could die. Her friends' refusal brought her to a new low because she could not even die on her own. Her miserable existence caused her to become bitter. Something happened one night that transformed her life into the beautiful, radiant Christian she is today.

Cindy, her best friend, was visiting her one night and trusting the Lord for some way to encourage Joni. Suddenly she spontaneously exclaimed, "Joni, Jesus knows how you feel. You're not the only one who's been paralyzed. He was paralyzed too!" Joni replied, "Cindy, what are you talking about?" "It's true. It's true, Joni. Remember, He was nailed to the cross. His back was raw from beatings like your back sometimes gets raw. Oh, He must have longed to move. To change His position, to redistribute His weight somehow, but He couldn't move. Joni, He knows how you feel."

This was the beginning of the breakthrough as the truth of this concept gripped Joni. She had never thought of it before. God's Son had felt the piercing sensation that racked her body. God's Son knew the helplessness she suffered. Joni later said, "God became incredibly close to me. I had seen what a difference the love shown me by friends and family had made. I began to realize that God also loved me."[6] It is of great value to realize that God not only knows and cares but also totally understands. Christ is "not a high priest who cannot sympathize with our weaknesses, but one who has been tempted in all things as we are, yet without sin" (Heb. 4:15). For this reason, we are encouraged to "draw near with confidence to the throne of grace, that we may receive mercy and find grace to help in time of need" (Heb. 4:16).

In our moments of despair, discouragement, loneliness, or any other kind of temptation, we can either turn these temptations into conversation with God, or we can attempt

---

[6] Phillip Yancey, *Where is God When It Hurts* (Grand Rapids, Zondervan), 118-119.

to deaden our pain by the temporary pleasure of sin, which carries bitter consequences. The Scriptures bear testimony of certain ones who have been greatly used of God and yet suffered such profound discouragement that they wanted to die! After Jonah preached the revival at Nineveh, his anger at God's compassion on his enemies drove him to the point of despair (Jonah 4:3). Fearless Elijah's amazing victory on Mount Carmel over the prophets of Baal was followed by such severe fear of Jezebel's threat that he asked the Lord to let him die (I Kings 19:1-4). Even our sinless Savior in his perfect humility was so grieved as He faced the prospect of the cross that He was tempted to rather die than live to carry out the Father's wishes. Our triumphant, compassionate Savior feels with us and desires to minister to us His understanding of our plight. Follow the example of the Psalmist in pouring out your heart to God:

My tears have been my food day and night,

While they say to me all day long, "Where is your God?"

These things I remember and I pour out my soul within me.

For I used to go along with the throng and lead them in procession to the house of God,

With the voice of joy and thanksgiving, a multitude keeping festival.

Why are you in despair, O my soul? And why have you become disturbed within me? Hope in God, for I shall again praise Him for the help of His presence. (Ps. 42:3-5)

Tom White, who directs a ministry to the persecuted church speaks of the understanding and companionship of the Son of God in the direst of circumstances when he writes, "When I was on trial in Cuba for the Gospel, with a machine gun behind me, the prosecutor made fun of me. I told him about Hebrews 12:1, which mentions the cloud of witnesses around me. Before trial I had been placed in special, cold cells with no furniture, no blanket, and no light. Cold air was blowing in above the door. Everything was taken from me. I began singing hymns and praise choruses. The guards got angry and pounded on the steel door with their fists. I was not destitute and alone. Second Corinthians 6:12 states that we can have nothing yet possess everything. I fellowshipped with the Creator of everything."[7]

There is unbearable pressure in the thought that we are alone. Jesus bore our punishment and the curse of separation from the Father when He died for us in order to give us the promise of His continual presence.

His Curse: "My God, my God, why hast Thou forsaken me" (Matt. 27:46).

Our Blessing: "I will never desert you, nor will I ever forsake you" (Heb. 13:5).

---

[7] *Jesus Freaks*, dcTalk and The Voice of the Martyrs (Tulsa, Okla.: Albury, 1999), 13.

In every part of life and ministry, there will be Someone with you who understands. Why not delight in the Lord's understanding of you at this very moment.

CHAPTER SEVEN

REJOICING IN THE RECONCILING HEART OF GOD AS YOU COME TO HIM IN PRAYER

The God who rules the world is never frantic as He carries out His eternal and loving plans. He is described as a God of peace (Rom. 15:33). However, there is one time that He is portrayed as being in a hurry! He is pictured as running to restore and reconcile His wayward people (Luke 15:20).

The story of the prodigal son is also the story of the reconciling father. The father is pictured as longingly waiting for the return of his runaway and rebellious son. The compassionate father ran to meet his son and embraced him and kissed him even before he made his confession (Luke 15:20-21)! The father is our Lord's portrayal of God rejoicing over the repentant heart and celebrating the restored relationship.

A modern story that parallels this story is about a young man named Sawat:

> Sawat had disgraced his family and dishonored his father's name. He had come to Bangkok to escape the dullness of village life. He had found excitement, and while he prospered in his sordid lifestyle he had found popularity as well.
>
> When he first arrived, he had visited a hotel unlike any he had ever seen. Every room had a window facing into the hallway, and in every room sat a girl. The older ones smiled and laughed. Others, just twelve or thirteen years old or younger, looked nervous, even frightened.
>
> That visit began Sawat's venture into Bangkok's world of prostitution. It began innocently enough, but he was quickly caught like a small piece of wood in a raging river. Its force was too powerful and swift for him, the current too strong.
>
> Soon he was selling opium to customers and propositioning tourists in the hotels. He even went so low as to actually help buy and sell young girls, some of them only nine and ten years old. It was a nasty business, and he was one of the most important of the young "businessmen."
>
> Then the bottom dropped out of his world: He hit a string of bad luck. He was robbed, and while trying to climb back to the top, he was arrested. The word went out in the underworld that he was a police spy.

He finally ended up living in a shanty by the city trash pile.

Sitting in his little shack, he thought about his family, especially his father, a simple Christian man from a small southern village near the Malaysian border. He remembered his dad's parting words: "I am waiting for you." He wondered whether his father would still be waiting for him after all that he had done to dishonor the family name. Would he be welcome in his home? Word of Sawat's lifestyle had long ago filtered back to the village.

Finally he devised a plan.

"Dear Father," he wrote, "I want to come home, but I don't know if you will receive me after all that I have done. I have sinned greatly, Father. Please forgive me. On Saturday night I will be on the train that goes through our village. If you are still waiting for me, will you tie a piece of cloth on the po tree in front of our house? (Signed) Sawat."

On that train he reflected on his life over the past few months and knew that his father had every right to deny him. As the train finally neared the village, he churned with anxiety. What would he do if there was no white cloth on the po tree?

Sitting opposite him was a kind stranger who had noticed how nervous his fellow passenger had become. Finally, Sawat could stand the pressure no longer. He blurted out his story in a torrent of words. As they entered the village, Sawat said, "Oh sir, I cannot bear to look. Can you watch for me? What if my father will not receive me back?"

Sawat buried his face in his knees. "Do you see it, sir? It's the only house with a po tree."

"Young man, your father did not hang just one piece of cloth. Look! He has covered the whole tree with cloth!" Sawat could hardly believe his eyes. The branches were laden with tiny white squares. In the front yard his old father jumped up and down, joyously waving a piece of white cloth, then ran in halting steps beside the train. When it stopped at the little station he threw his arms around his son, embracing him with tears of joy. "I've been waiting for you!" he exclaimed.[8]

We do not base our theology and our thinking about God on our experience or anybody else's. However, while our theology should be based solely on the Word of God, it is also to be brought into our experiences. God is One who responds to a repentant heart. Christ even anticipated and predicted the apostle Peter's denial of Him and at the same time prayed for him and anticipated His restoration. Satan will attempt to turn one failure into a lifetime of failure, but God desires otherwise:

> Simon, Simon, behold, Satan has demanded permission to sift you like wheat; but I have prayed for

---

[8] Floyd McClung, *The Father Heart of God* (Eugene, Ore.: Harvest House, 1985), 111-114.

you, that your faith may not fail; and you, when once
you have turned again, strengthen your brothers. (Luke
22:31-32)

Once a person has confessed and forsaken his sin, God is
eager to restore him. This is not to say that there are no
consequences for one's sins, but it is to say that the Lord
will give one an opportunity to affirm a renewed love for
Him (John 21:15-17). To a repentant heart God is even able
to work together for good, one's past sin (Rom 8:28). While
an unrepentant heart can greatly abuse this truth, a
repentant heart desperately needs to be forgiven,
comforted, and reaffirmed. If this does not happen, one can
be "overwhelmed by excessive sorrow" (2 Cor. 2:7).

In James 4 God refers to His unfaithful children as
adulteresses (James 4:4)! The invitation that He gives to
those who have abandoned Him and made Him their enemy
is to "draw near to God and He will draw near to you"
(James 4:8). God is the most reconciling person with whom
we will ever have a relationship. Come to Him today!

He who conceals his transgressions will not prosper,
But he who confesses and forsakes them will find
compassion. (Prov. 28:13)

CHAPTER EIGHT

EXPERIENCING FREEDOM FROM THE FEAR OF MAN THROUGH PRAYER

I had returned on Saturday evening from a three-week trip to the Middle East. It had been a glorious time, but even more glorious was the Scripture that the Lord illuminated to my spirit on the following Sunday morning in my apartment in Wheaton, Illinois. 1 Corinthians 9:19 leaped off the page as I read these words:

> For though I am free from all men, I have made myself a slave to all, that I might win the more. (1 Cor. 9:19)

The phrase in this verse that struck me was not that I was to be a servant or slave to all. I knew that, even though I confessed I was not a very good one. It was the truth of being "free from all men", that the Spirit of God underlined that Sunday morning. In fact, it started a spiritual journey in which I spent a year asking God to show me the implication of this truth for my life. After the year of seeking God I came to the following conclusions:

It Implies a Freedom from Letting the Expectations of Others be the Lord of Your Life.

The apostle Paul told the church to imitate him as he imitated Christ. Christ had the freedom to stop and spend time with the Father even when the crowds were demanding His presence and ministry (Mark 1:35-38). If one genuinely loves God, he will also love people. However, it is a misguided theology that requires one to love the world more than God. There is a difference between making wise choices that are based on our knowledge of God's will and making choices that are solely based on the demands of others. Listen to this analysis of the humorous but sometimes truthful description of a pastor's plight:

The pastor of a church is in a precarious position; he can't please everyone! It has been said:

- If he is young, he lacks experience; if his hair is gray, he's too old for the young people.

- If he has several children, he has too many; if he has no children, he's setting a bad example.

- If he preaches from his notes, he has canned sermons and is too dry; if he doesn't use notes, he has not studied and is not deep.

- If he is attentive to the poor people in the church, they claim he is playing to the grandstand; if he pays attention to the wealthy, he is trying to be an aristocrat.

- If he suggests changes for improvement of the church, he is a dictator; if he makes no suggestions, he is a figurehead.

- If he uses too many illustrations, he neglects the Bible; if he doesn't use enough illustrations, he isn't clear.

- If he condemns wrong, he is cranky; if he doesn't preach against sin, he's a compromiser.

- If he preaches the truth, he's offensive; if he doesn't preach the truth, he's a hypocrite.

- If he fails to please somebody, he's hurting the church and ought to leave; if he tries to please everyone, he is a fool.

- If he preaches about money, he's a money grabber; if he doesn't preach spiritual giving, he is failing to develop the people.

- If he drives an old car, he shames his congregation; if he drives a new car, he is setting his affection on earthly things.

- If he preaches all the time, the people get tired of hearing one man; if he invites guest speakers, he is shirking his responsibility.

- If he receives a large salary, he's a mercenary; if he receives only a small salary, well—it proves he isn't worth much anyway.

—Author Unknown

As David Hansen has wisely said, "What must die in every pastor is the subconscious desire to please people. What must not die is the will to love." Paul's freedom led him to be a servant to people by serving God. It was for this reason that he said, "If I were still trying to please men, I would not be a bondservant of Christ" (Gal. 1:10). As P.F. Forsyth said, "The ideal minister must love and understand people but must know and love more the will and word of God."

Freedom from letting the expectations of others become the Lord of our life releases us to experience the grace of prayer and ministry, looking to the Lord to meet the deepest desires of the heart as we are led by Him. It opens up time for the Lord to care for you and keep you refreshed. Yeses and Noes are both in the will of God. Anne Lamott gave the following advice to a graduating seminary class: "We don't want you to talk about this being the day the Lord has made and that we should rejoice and savor its beauty and poignancy when secretly you're tearing around like a white rabbit; we need you to walk the walk. And we need you to walk a little more slowly."

It Implies Freedom from Letting the Responses of People be the Basis of Your Joy in the Lord.

When the woman lovingly poured her expensive perfume over Jesus as an act of sacrificial service, what was the response of the people? They called it a waste and scolded her:

> But some were indignantly remarking to one another, "Why has this perfume been wasted?" For this perfume might have been sold for over three hundred denarii, and the money given to the poor." And they were scolding her. (Mark 14:4-5)

What was our Lord's response?

> But Jesus said, "Let her alone; why do you bother her? She has done a good deed to Me. For you always have the poor with you, and whenever you wish you can do good to them; but you do not always have Me. She has done what she could; she has anointed My body beforehand for the burial. Truly I say to you, wherever the gospel is preached in the whole world, what this woman has done will also be spoken of in memory of her." (Mark 14:6-9)

Man's response often tells us that prayer and ministry is a waste. We need to learn to listen to the Lord who finds delight in the prayers of the righteous (Prov. 15:8) and tells us that our labor is not in vain (1 Cor. 15:58).

Jesus felt a great love for a young man who came up to Him one day and questioned Him about how to obtain eternal life. In order to allow him to see that his god was his money and see a need for repentance, the Lord lovingly showed him his point of resistance:

> Looking at him, Jesus felt a love for him and said to him, "One thing you lack: go and sell all you possess and give to the poor, and you will have treasure in heaven; and come, follow Me." (Mark 10:21)

The man's response to Jesus' great love was grief:

> But at these words he was saddened and went away grieving, for he was one who owned much property. (Mark 10:22)

Jesus did not base the success of His actions on man's response but rather the response of His heavenly Father. In our Lord's greatest time of crisis in His earthly life He chose three of His closest companions to pray with Him in the garden of Gethsemane. He found them sleeping (Mark 14:37) and later all fleeing from Him (Mark 14:50). However, His heavenly Father stood with Him and prepared and enabled Him for His upcoming death. He can sustain you even when your closest companions let you down.

The woman who anointed Christ had to make a choice: she could listen to the scolding and ridicule, or the affirmation of Christ. Christ also had to listen to His heavenly Father for the evaluation of His ministry when even His love was not met with an appreciative response. This enabled Him to say:

> I glorified You on the earth, having accomplished the work which You have given Me to do. (John 17:4)

The grace of God can empower you to be successful in this way and to aid the true successes of others.

We are free from letting man's response be our basis of joy in the Lord. This freedom enables us to love others in a responsible way and also discern the limits of this responsibility. As Romans 12:18 states:

> If possible, so far as it depends on you, be at peace with all men. (Rom. 12:18)

One dear friend shared with me the frustration he felt every time he spent time with an older man he deeply respected. He said, "It seems that he is never pleased with anything I say or do. I always walk away feeling so helpless of ever being able to please or encourage him." The lie that he had to reject was: "I am responsible to make this man happy." It had to be replaced with: "I am responsible to be a channel of the Lord's love to this man. I desire him to respond but his response is beyond my control." The grace of God leads to success and freedom in living before God.

One who is free is able to take loving risks even in relationships. The apostle Paul had an enormous capacity for relationships. The security that a believer in Christ can know is that even if man fails us, the Lord will not! Listen to Paul's testimony:

> At my first defense no one supported me, but all deserted me; may it not be counted against them. But the Lord stood with me and strengthened me, so that through me the proclamation might be fully accomplished, and that all the Gentiles might hear; and I was rescued out of the lion's mouth. The Lord will rescue me from every evil deed, and will bring me safely to His heavenly kingdom; to Him be the glory forever and ever. Amen. (2 Tim. 4:16-18)

The German Reformer Martin Luther was asked one day, "Where would you be if all your followers were to leave you." His response: "I would be right in the very hands of God." Since none of us is really in competition with anyone else, would you be willing to pray, "Lord, make me into the freest man or the freest woman alive. Lead me into the freedom to live before you and to be led by you as my gracious and kind Master."? Pray that you can be used of God to aid many others to experience this same freedom. The next chapters may be the beginning of the answer to this prayer.

CHAPTER NINE

EXPERIENCING THE FREEDOM TO LIVE BEFORE GOD

A few hundred years ago an accomplished European pianist gave a concert before thousands of people in a prestigious music hall. After he performed one of his famous pieces the audience rose to their feet. Their thunderous applause filled the concert hall. He was later asked to express his emotional response to this occasion. Most expected him to say that it was the greatest experience of his life. He replied, "I liked the applause, but it wasn't the most important thing to me. After the audience had sat down I noticed my teacher of thirty years sitting in the top corner of the balcony. He looked at me and he gave me a nod of approval. That one nod from my master brought me more pleasure than the standing ovation of thousands."[9]

The pianist had learned to live before an audience of one. The Lord Jesus reflected this pursuit when He stated, "And

---

[9] S.J. Hill, *Enjoying God* (Lake Mary, Florida: Relevant Books, 2001), 70.

He who sent me is with me; He has not left me alone, for I always do the things that are pleasing to Him" (John 8:29).

Can you imagine the freedom that could come into your life if you caught a glimpse of God and began to live before Him? I heard David Bryant remark that the church has the people and the resources to have evangelized the world one thousand times over. God's people need to experience the freedom of Christ in order that His love can be unleashed through them in true service.

Richard Foster has written about the difference between a self-righteous service and true service.[10] The following is one attempt to summarize some of these differences:

FALSE	**TRUE**
Frantic scheming is energy of the flesh	Calmness of spirit in response to the prompting of the Spirit
Needs human attention	Does not fear attention but does not seek it either-- content with God's approval

[10] Richard Foster, *Celebration of Discipline* (San Francisco: Harper and Row, 1978), 112.

FALSE	**TRUE**
Overly concerned with results	Delights in the service and able to serve one's enemies and friends as the Lord directs
"Performs" acts of service without sensitivity	Serves as a lifestyle in sensitivity to Holy Spirit and the opportune moment
Tries to make people feel indebted	Builds freedom in relationships

When God's love begins to control us, its passionate hold on us will overflow to those around us. One who is taught of the Spirit and led by the Spirit will begin to love as God loves. Rivers of living water will begin to flow through the one who continually takes his needy heart to the Lord alone to quench his thirsts (John 7:37-39).

Such living before God will begin to affect our marriage and other close relationships. As we live before God, the Lord can extend His love, acceptance, and freedom to others. It enables us to rejoice at other's differences, interests, and successes. It also gives us an appropriate freedom from the other person, so as not to try to do everything for them and take undue responsibility for their happiness. Such freedom enables us to not unduly react to their feelings and responses and lovingly live before the Lord. This freedom makes it possible to enjoy true intimacy in working, playing, and serving God together. It also provides the opportunity to talk about our differences, express our feelings, and experience emotional support.

The freedom of living before God will transform and purify the motivation for spiritual leadership. A true spiritual leader will not emphasize his rights and seek to control others but rather his responsibility to equip others to trust God. This kind of leader is more concerned with heart attitude and brokenness before God rather than outward activities and group conformity. A true spiritual leader will not stress the uniqueness of "his" group but rather the importance of the unity of the whole body of Christ. God works through such leaders to create an atmosphere of love, trust, and service of belonging because they are included in important decisions. An atmosphere of concern, affirmation, peace, and thankfulness for God is seen as the source of everything.

In this freedom of living before God, we must face the reality that while human relationships are vital in our lives, they cannot give us the love that we crave and need. In the midst of all of our relationships we must learn to drink from Christ—the source of all true love (John 7:37). Determine to trust God, so that you will not leave this chapter without placing yourself on God's altar and asking Him to do whatever it takes to lead you into this glorious freedom. Let Him love you at your points of guilt, fear, and anger. He knows you and me and sent His Son to die for us. We can trust Him to honor His name by leading us into the freedom of the grace of prayer that Jesus purchased for us on the cross. Allowing God to do a work in you is the first step in allowing Him to work through you as a soul physician.

CHAPTER TEN

SEEING THE CONSEQUENCES OF FAILING TO EXPERIENCE GOD'S DELIGHT

Gracious Acceptance in Christ

As long as you look at this truth of God's gracious acceptance in Christ as only something nice, you have not quite grasped it. It is not just nice; it is utterly necessary. To fail to digest this truth is to live under the motivation of fear—the fear of rejection and failure. This is what motivates most of the people to whom you will seek to minister.

Ask God to show you those things in your life which you do, or do not do, say, or do not say, that flow out of a fear of rejection. In God's great kindness He can show you why you want well-behaved children, why you desire a better home or car, why you work overtime, or why you keep a neat house or yard. Every unhealthy addiction is rooted in a lack of understanding of this truth.

Jesus provides a love and acceptance for you, and His Spirit is able to witness the reality of this love to your spirit so that you can rest in it. Everyone yearns to hear, "This is my beloved Son in whom I am well pleased." We need this affirmation that the Father spoke to His Son. In Jesus we have this affirmation—the Father loves us with the same intensity as He loves His Son (John 17:23)! His love for you is just as intense at this moment as it was when Jesus was dying on the cross for you. His love is eternal and unchanging, and you can rest in it.

When you rest in this love and focus upon it, you are freed to achieve what God has for you to do. A parent is not able to discipline his children with the appropriate tenderness and firmness if he finds himself looking to his children to provide the acceptance that can be found only in God. Husbands and wives cannot fulfill God's desire to their mate if they try to ultimately find in them the love and acceptance they need. A man may make a good husband but he will always make a lousy god. A woman may make a good wife but she will always make a lousy god. A job can be a legitimate means to receive God's provision and to serve Him, but it also will make a lousy god. Only God--not any other person, position, or possession--can meet the thirst of our heart: to be loved and accepted.

Many believers are chained to sin habits in their lives because, in order to experience Christ's freedom, they need to humble themselves before another, confess their bondage and ask for help. It is fear of what this other one might think that keeps them in chains. Others of us fail to ever be an effective witness for Christ because of our fear of what people might think if we were to tell them about our

Lord. Still others of us pursue materialism and make unneeded purchases to meet the thirsts of our empty hearts that crave to be satisfied with Christ's love.[11]

John Regier is a Biblical counselor in Colorado Springs. He related the story of a couple who married in college, went to seminary, and then entered a pastoral ministry. Diane had grown up in the home of an alcoholic father and a dominant mother. She had learned to cope with her feelings of rejection by keeping them inside her and trying to bury them as her dominant mother did. Mark had grown up in the home of a successful attorney who had high expectations for his son. Mark never felt like he did anything right in his father's eyes but was determined to show his dad that he could be successful.

Mark spent very long hours in his ministry as he visited the people, counseled them in their needs, and sought to prepare excellent messages. The words of his dad constantly ran through his mind, "Son you will always be a failure; you can't do anything right." His greatest desire was to prove his dad wrong.

Diane became frustrated that her husband never had time to be at home anymore. She channeled her energy into the children and grew distant from Mark. Her husband continued to work hard, and as the church grew he felt that perhaps he was proving his dad wrong.

Mark and Diane attended a conference to teach them how to help couples solve their marriage difficulties. In the process they began to become aware of their own! Diane got in touch with her buried feelings of rejection by her

---

[11] I am indebted to Del Fehsenfeld's message, *The Fear of Man*

parents and also of her bitterness toward her husband's workaholism. Mark began to realize that his drive to be successful was controlling his life and destroying his relationships with the Lord and with his family. He became aware of his need to forgive his father for telling him that he would be a failure, and for the pressure to perform that this had produced. Now Mark understood the he had greatly damaged his wife and in tears of repentance asked her forgiveness. She asked his forgiveness for her critical attitude and began to experience a growing oneness with her husband. Mark returned to his work with a new outlook. He began to focus on loving his wife and the people that God had entrusted to his care—no longer on "his" goals that would prove him successful. His messages began to come from his heart and God's clear blessing was seen on his life, family, and ministry.

What is the most important responsibility that God has given His creation? According to Jesus' teaching it is to respond to His love and love Him with our entire being (Matt. 22:37-39). The Bible makes it clear that any communication, spiritual gift, knowledge and insight, miraculous faith, or sacrificial service that is not motivated by love is absolutely worthless (I Cor. 13:1-3). If love is this essential and if our love is only a response to knowing His love for us, what is more important than knowing His love for you?

One year I asked God to overwhelm me with His love, so that I could better respond in loving Him. To be overwhelmed with God's love is to realize that He loves us in a way that no one else ever will or can. I still have the sheets of paper where I kept the insights God gave me in

1984 in regard to His amazing love. Familiar passages opened up to me in fresh ways.

To whom did Christ show His love, according to Romans 5:6-10? It was to the "helpless," "ungodly," "sinners," and His "enemies." One summer day of 1984 I "felt" particularly "ungodly" in my attitudes. I also sensed His love for an ungodly man in a way I never had before. Many times I have felt "helpless" and experienced God's love for me in my helpless state. If God so loved us this way when we were His enemies, will He make us perform for His love now that we are His reconciled friends?

Every time I saw a passage that showed me my responsibility to love, I would ask, "How is it that the Lord has first loved me in this way?" For example, Proverbs 17:9 says, "He who covers a transgression seeks love, but he who repeats a matter separates intimate friends." I reasoned, "Thank You Lord that You offer me Your gracious forgiveness because You are seeking to build a relationship of love." If God constantly rubbed all of our failures in our face, we would never enjoy an intimate relationship with Him. God desires us to imitate Him in our relationship with others and offer loving forgiveness rather than reminding them of all their failures.

It is God's loving acceptance that provides a genuine believer with a place of rest. Rightly understand, you can never overemphasize this resting truth of God's loving acceptance. It is an absolutely necessary foundation for the development of the Christian life. You will never find the love, understanding, appreciation, or affirmation you need outside of Christ, Who is the Giver of every good and perfect gift. He is better than the best of men (Rom. 5:7-8).

When you are struggling, you can rest in this love as you call upon Him. When you feel inadequate, you can rest in His loving adequacy. In any and all circumstances you can rest in His holy love.

Wherever you have come from and wherever you are today, there is restoration for you to be found in the loving arms of the Lord of the universe. His love can become your delight and He can satisfy your thirsty soul. In the Lord Jesus' love you can find "rest for **your** soul." Is this the day that you are being prompted to come to God and ask Him to overwhelm you with His loving acceptance and to enter into a deeper experience of the grace of prayer? Trusting God to do this for you is the most important step in being a channel of this love for others as an effective soul physician.

CHAPTER ELEVEN

BEING AMBITIOUS TO RECEIVE THE GIFT OF GOD'S GRACIOUS REST

The story of Mary and Martha in Luke 10:38-42 is not chronologically related to the accounts that precede it and follow it. The inspired placement of this delightful passage is thematic rather than chronological. The spontaneous loving compassion that is seen in the preceding story of the Good Samaritan is the fruit of the restful spirit that the Lord commends in Mary. The anxious spirit of Martha chokes this loving compassion. The restful communion is the very attitude that gives birth to a prayerful delight in God (Luke 11:1-13). On the other hand, a hurried spirit is the death of prayer. Jesus looked at people and felt with them in their worried and anxious state. He invited them to come to Him and share in what He called "rest for [the soul]" (Matt. 11:29). It is this rest that He is graciously offering you today! It is a gift of God that will bring great pleasure to God as He observes you enjoying His grace. Countless people will thank God for you throughout eternity if you take the time to learn from Christ about this gift.

It is not only a rest from the guilt of sin and the hope of living with God in heaven for all eternity in an environment of perfect peace, but also a rest in this present life amidst all of your conflicts, stress, and trials. It is a "rest" that makes possible a life of love for others, a genuine, prayerful delight in God, and a life of eternal significance. When you purpose to discover this gift you are choosing something truly "good" (which cannot be taken away from you [Luke 10:42]), and experiencing the grace of God.

I had been asked to be one of the speakers for a special series of meetings at Moody Bible Institute designed to motivate the students to be involved in evangelism. In order to prepare for the opportunity, I walked down the street from my office to a restaurant and ordered a cup of coffee. With my pen and pencil in hand and an open Bible I sought God concerning what He would have me to say. Finding myself fretting over my desire for some direction, I began to look around at some of the other customers at their tables. In my state of anxiety I realized that I did not have the slightest feeling of compassion for their souls even though I was seeking to give an inspirational message on evangelism. Strangely enough it was at this moment that God gave me direction on what to speak as He brought to mind a verse of Scripture.

An Honorable Ambition

What are your ambitions? What do you desire to achieve in this life? One ambition that the believer in Christ is encouraged to cultivate is the ambition to lead a quiet or peaceful life (I Thess. 4:11). This is the verse that the Lord brought to mind that day in the restaurant. The Greek word in this verse that is translated "make it your ambition", is used two other times in the New Testament and refers to Paul's personal aspiration to please the Lord (2 Cor. 5:9) and to preach the gospel where it has never been preached (Rom. 15:20).

A student once wrote the following quotation on a sheet of paper and gave it to me. The only documentation on it was that it was from a 16th century saint. Listen to a portion of it, for it has relevance to our modern world:

> Strive to see God in all things without exception, and acquiesce in His will with absolute submission. Do everything for God, uniting yourself to Him by a more upward glance, or by the overflowing of your heart towards Him. Never be in a hurry; do everything quietly and in a calm spirit. Do not lose your inward peace for anything whatsoever, even if your whole world seems upset. Commend all to God, and then lie still and be at rest in His bosom. Whatever happens, abide steadfast in a determination to cling simply to God, trusting in His eternal love for you; and if you find that you have wandered forth from His shelter, recall your heart quietly and simply. Maintain a holy simplicity of mind and do not smother yourself with a host of cares, wishes, or longings, under any pretext. (Source unknown)

At first glance the aspiration of a life of peace may appear to be self-centered, unrealistic, and unproductive. However, the ambition of pursuing a life of peace is consistent with pleasing God (2 Cor. 5:9), and being used as a vessel of His love for others (Rom. 15:20). Jesus called this honorable ambition of pursuing a life of rest "good" and that which leads to eternal accomplishments (Luke 10:42). The absence of this peace leads to being distracted, doubting God's care, and a demanding spirit (Luke 10:40-41). It is for this reason that it invites our Lord's loving rebuke similar to His kind command: "Be anxious for nothing" (Phil. 4:6).

Would you be willing to let God search your heart and reveal to you any concern or care that you have not cast upon Him? God does not stop with the command, "Be anxious for nothing," but shows us how to process this anxiety with prayer. Right now, talk to God about any anxiety, tell Him what you would like for Him to do about it, and do not forget to thank Him that He is so eager to bear your burdens.[12] May you purpose to live a life that fully obeys 1 Peter 5:7—"casting all your anxiety upon Him." May God mightily work through you—even your weakness--to help many others experience this rest for their souls.

---

[12] For further development of this idea, see my book: *A Journey to Victorious Praying.* (Chicago: Moody Press, 2003) pgs. 177-185.

CHAPTER TWELVE

UNDERSTANDING OUR NEED AND GOD'S PROVISION TO LIBERATE OUR LIVES

David Seamonds relates the following story of a godly minister as he writes:

> Some years ago I received a phone call from the wife of a minister friend of mine, asking me to counsel her husband who had just suffered a complete nervous breakdown. As we were driving to the hospital, she began to talk about him. "I just don't understand Bill. It's almost as if he has a built-in slave drive that won't let him go. He can't relax, can't let down. He's always overworking. His people just love him; and they would do anything for him, but he can't let them. He's gone on and on like this for so many years that finally he has broken completely."

I began to visit with Bill, and after he was well enough to talk, he shared with me about his home and childhood. As Bill grew up he wanted very much to please his parents. He tried to win his mother's approval by occasionally helping her set the table. But she'd say, "Bill you've got the knives in the wrong place." After that it would be the salad plates. He could never please her. Try as hard as he might, he could never please his father either. He brought home his report card with B's and C's. His dad looked at the card and said, "Bill, I think if you try, you could surely get all B's couldn't you?" So he studied harder and harder, until one day he brought home all B's. Dad said, "But surely you know if you just put a little more effort into it, you could get all A's." So he worked and struggled through a semester or two, until finally he got all A's. He was so excited-- now Mother and Dad would surely be pleased with him. He ran home, for he could hardly wait. Dad looked at the report card and said, "Well I know those teachers. They always give A's."

When Bill became a minister, all he did was exchange one mother and father for several hundred of them: his congregation became his unappeasable parents. He could never satisfy them, no matter what he did. Finally, he just collapsed under the sheer weight of struggling for approval and trying to prove himself.[13]

---

[13] David Seamonds, *Healing for Damaged Emotions*, (Wheaton: Victor, 1981), 16-17.

A college friend of mine came up to me and spontaneously offered this insight about himself when he stated, "I may not have as high a moral standard as you; but I can't even live up to mine. Why would I want to become a Christian and adopt your standards that would make me feel even more condemned?" I responded by attempting to explain this precious resting truth that we have explored in these preceding chapters.

The Need for Meditation

There is a difference between mentally acknowledging a truth and resting in that same truth. It is probable that Bill, in the opening illustration, acknowledged and even preached the truth that we will look at in this chapter. He may have even assured others of its truth, but he certainly was not resting in it. Jesus spoke of His words abiding or living in us (John 15:7). Romans 8:16 refers to the Holy Spirit witnessing with the believer's spirit of the truth that God is his Father and he is God's child. Paul prayed that the Colossian Christians would be filled or controlled with God's truth (Col. 1:9).

In our age of "information explosion" we could almost drown in the knowledge to which we are constantly exposed. In its own way this excessive amount of information hinders the communication process. It is very difficult to effectively communicate spiritual truth that does not live in you (John 15:7) and fill or control you (Col. 1:9). It is for this reason that John Wesley, the early Methodist leader, instructed his men, "Don't go out to preach until you 'know' your sins are forgiven." Meditation upon the

Scriptures allows the Holy Spirit to illuminate our minds, refocus our emotions, and redirect our wills.[14]

Understanding our True Condition

When we acknowledge our sin and rebellion against the Lord and turn to Christ in faith, we enter into a covenant relationship with God. We enter into what the Scriptures call the New Covenant. This covenant was first given to believers in the nation of Israel and can be found in such passages as Ezekiel 36. God has covenanted or solemnly promised to do certain things for His people who come to Him in faith. One of these promises is found in Ezekiel 36:25, "Then I will sprinkle clean water on you, and you will be clean; I will cleanse you from all your filthiness and from all your idols." This word picture of cleansing describes God's gracious forgiveness that allows one to be perfectly accepted by a loving and holy God.

I recall the great struggle that a lady, who was a pastor's wife, was having concerning her past sin. She finally confided in a dear friend of mine who was able to greatly help her. She told him, "I come to church week after week and feel so unworthy to praise God. The other people are worthy, but I am not. I have the memory of the abortion of my baby every time I seek to worship God." He responded, "You are actually a whole lot worse off than you think you are." You are probably asking, "How did that help her?" He pointed out she was controlled by the thought: "If I didn't

---

[14] In my book *Living the Life God Has Planned--A Guide to Knowing God's Will*, Moody Press, I discuss how to develop the habit of meditation in your life pp. 162-167.

have this past abortion, I would be worthy to praise God."
My friend showed her how greatly we have all fallen short
of God's holy standards. Sin is lawlessness according to I
John 3:4.

- Have you always loved God above all else?

- Have you ever looked to someone or something
  other than God to meet the desires of your heart?
  (This is idolatry.)

- Have you ever failed to honor God's name or
  reputation?

- Have you ever failed to honor your parents?

- Have you ever gotten angry at someone and
  hated them? (The Bible calls this murder Matt.
  5:21-22.)

- Have you ever stolen anything? (Ballpoint pen,
  employer's time, etc.)

- Have you ever lied?

- Have you ever expressed discontentment and
  coveted what belonged to another?

God in His perfect holiness must punish sin by His wrath. If
you are guilty of breaking one commandment you are a
lawbreaker and guilty of all (James 2:10). If you compare
your life to Adolph Hitler's, you may feel very good about
yourself. However, honestly look at yourself in light of
God's holiness; we can agree that we are "filthy" and

"idolaters."[15] Only when our mouths are shut are we able to look to God's solutions (Rom. 3:19-20).

The Provision of God's Loving and Acceptance and Delight

Jesus Christ came to earth and bore our just condemnation. His death was a sufficient payment for our sins and is able to deliver one from God's wrath to the experience of God's love, acceptance, and delight. This dear pastor's wife found freedom and relief in God's covenant promise to cleanse her from all her filthiness and idolatry. In her mind she knew the truth, but now she began to rest in it.

The apostle Paul made it clear that he was a minister of this New Covenant (2 Cor. 3:5-6) and this covenant promise of God's loving cleansing originally given to Israel has a definite application to every believer in Christ. Every person who acknowledges their sin and puts their faith in Christ is no longer condemned by God's wrath but justified by His grace and stands in this grace (Rom. 5:2).

The foundation to experiencing the grace of ministry and prayer is to cease trying to find a reason inside of yourself for God to bless you. Realize that apart from Christ, you are bankrupt before God. Humble yourself before Him and enjoy what you can never earn or will ever deserve--His gracious acceptance. This is the only acceptable foundation, and any other one will lead to spiritual bondage and ultimately defeat your life.

---

[15] I am indebted to the teaching of Ray Comfort who has clearly communicated how God's moral law exposes man's sin.

SECTION TWO

Need for Hope in Your Struggles—Experiencing the Grace of Hope in Christ

There is a battle going on inside of every believer whom you will ever meet. One not only needs to understand this battle but also to understand the biblical solution that makes possible a life of continual victory.

This section is designed to help you understand your identity in Christ in a way that will enable you to experience hope in your greatest struggle. Are you viewing yourself in the way God sees you? Would you like to be able to guide others into replacing their despair with hope? Would you like to know the basis of overcoming "lifelong strongholds"? Would you like to overcome boredom and experience true fulfillment?

This section is designed to help you in your journey to answer these questions in your life and also to equip you to help others in their journey.

CHAPTER THIRTEEN

BUILDING ON THE RIGHT FOUNDATION

Every believer has the principle of sin with which to contend. Many have chosen to designate this principle by calling it the believer's "sin nature" while others sense that this terminology is not the best way to describe it. The Bible uses the terms "flesh" and "indwelling sin". Whatever you call it, there is a battle going on inside of every Christian. How do we experience and lead others to a victorious Christian experience in light of this battle?

It is healthy to recognize that this battle is related to one's "flesh". Many "Christian" teachings appeal to getting the flesh to conform to certain outward habits. However, the first step is to recognize the rotten nature of the "flesh" (cf. Rom. 7:18) and to ask the Lord to show you how it seeks to manifest itself in your life. The "flesh" is one's capacity to live life independent of God. Listen to the words of a publication entitled "Traits of the Self-life":

The flesh or the self is so much a part of our thinking that we often do not even recognize its presence. Just in case you still think that you may have escaped its influence, here are some questions to ask yourself.

Are you ever conscious of:

- A secret spirit of pride; an exalted feeling in view of your success of position, because of your good training and appearance, because of your natural gifts and abilities; an important independent spirit; stiffness and preciseness.

- The stirrings of anger or impatience, which, worst of all, you call nervousness or holy indignation; a touchy, sensitive spirit; a disposition which dislikes being contradicted; a desire to throw sharp, heated words at another.

- Self-will; a stubborn, unteachable spirit; an arguing, talkative spirit; harsh, sarcastic expressions; an unyielding, headstrong disposition; a driving, commanding spirit; a disposition to criticize and pick flaws when set aside and unnoticed; a peevish, fretful spirit; a disposition that loves to be coaxed and humored.

- Carnal fear; a man-fearing spirit; a shrinking from reproach and duty; reasoning around your cross; a shrinking from doing your whole duty by those of wealth or position; a fearfulness that someone will offend and drive some prominent person away; a compromising spirit.

- A jealous disposition; a secret spirit of envy shut up in your heart; an unpleasant sensation in view of the great prosperity and success of another; a disposition to speak of the faults and failings rather than the gifts and virtues of those more talented and appreciated than yourself.

- A dishonest, deceitful disposition; the evading and covering of the truth; the covering up of your real faults; the leaving of a better impression of yourself than is strictly true; false humility; exaggeration; straining the truth.

- Unbelief; a spirit of discouragement in times of pressure; lack of faith and trust in God; a disposition to worry and complain in the midst of pain, poverty, or at the dispensations of Divine Providence; an over anxious feeling about whether everything will come out all right.

- Formality and deadness, lack of concern for lost souls; dryness and indifference; lack of power with God.[16]

The Bible clearly teaches that it is possible for the believer to live in daily victory in the strength of Christ. What is the proper foundation for a victorious prayer life? Is it:

A. Desire — "You have to truly want it."

B. Determination — "You have to be **determined** to get it."

---

[16] *Traits of the Self-Life*, (Saskatoon, Saskatchewan, Canada: Western Tract Missions)

    C. Discipline — "You need to discipline yourself to get it."

Desire is important because Jesus himself asked a man that he healed, "Do you wish to get well?" (John 5:6)

Determination is unquestionably a Christ-like quality as evidenced in our Lord's words: "My food is to do the will of Him who sent me and to accomplish His work" (John 4:34).

Discipline is a necessary ingredient in the Christian life, and Paul speaks not only of "buffeting [his] body" (1 Cor. 9:27) but also of sowing to the Spirit and not the flesh (Gal. 6:8).

However, as important as desires, determination and discipline are, they are not the foundation. The foundation is CHRIST! It is the simplicity of this foundation which causes many to stumble in regard to the Christian life. A wrong foundation can cause one to look within to find the victory and leads to despair when we have a hard day.

Before a person becomes a Christian he must first see his helpless condition and total inadequacy to save himself from his plight. As we see in of Romans 3:19 his mouth must be shut because he has no righteousness of his own. He realizes that he has not lived up to God's holy Law and deserves the consequences of His eternal wrath.

After a person has realized his need, he can then be illuminated to see the adequacy and sufficiency of Christ. His death and resurrection is **the** answer to his need. When one trusts Christ, miraculous things happen. Lewis Sperry Chafer once took a vacation with the purpose of studying the New Testament to note what happens at salvation. He noted thirty-three things that happen to a person when they trust Christ!

This same faith is involved in living the Christian life. One must first come to realize his complete inability to live the life God has called us to live. Our spiritual enemies are too powerful for us and the standards are too high to attain through our own efforts. The **only** answer to our predicament is Jesus Christ and His finished work. We must trust God alone on the basis of Christ's death and resurrection. When we do, the Spirit of God is released to work in and through our lives. The same faith that we exercised at the point of initial salvation is the faith that is necessary to live the Christian life. The object of this faith is Jesus Christ and His finished work (Col. 2:6)!

As a new father who had just discovered that God had miraculously created a little one in the womb of my wife, I eagerly sought God to learn how to embark on this new journey. I received some "unusual" advice to talk to the baby and read Scripture to it during the months prior to the birth. I read some amazing things about the life of the unborn, even how things that they are exposed to in the womb are things that they have a greater disposition for after birth. I did not know if this was true, but Penny and I thought that it sure would not hurt, and we sought to follow this advice. Day after day I read the Bible to "little one" as I called him—book after book of the Scriptures.

The exercise of reading the Scripture to the child reaped a number of immediate benefits. First of all, after talking to them for nine months, when they are born, you feel like you are meeting an old friend. Secondly, their hearing develops at about four months, and so they learn to recognize your voice. In the birthing room at the hospital the fetal monitor hooked up to the baby showed his heart beat getting quite high. As I said, "It's OK little one, it's OK," the heartbeat did in this case go down!

One evening as I was about to read the Gospel of Luke to "little one," an insight flashed into my mind. I believe it was an answer to my prayer of many years to better understand what it means to be "in Christ". My instant instinct was to stop reading Luke and turn to Colossians 3:1-4:

> Therefore if you have been raised up with Christ, keep seeking the things above, where Christ is, seated at the right hand of God. Set your mind on the things above, not on the things that are on earth. For you have died and your life is hidden with Christ in God. When Christ, who is our life, is revealed, then you also will be revealed with Him in glory. (Col. 3:1-4)

The insight that "hit" me was that the idea of being "in Christ" should not be a mystery to us. All of our lives started out inside of another person. Every person's life begins inside his mother. Furthermore, nor should it be hard to grasp the idea of the actions of the person we are living inside, having a practical effect upon us. All of us experienced it inside our mother. When our mothers ate, we got nourished. Other amazing studies have even revealed the effect of the mother's attitude on the baby inside her.

The Bible teaches very clearly that when one becomes a Christian he enjoys a spiritual union with Christ which is described as being "baptized into Christ" (Rom. 6:3). The result is that the actions of His death and resurrection have a practical effect upon us. We are united with Christ in His death and resurrection (Rom. 6:5).

What is the practical effect of being united with Christ in His death? His death not only satisfied God's righteousness and freed the believer from the guilt of sin but also liberates him from the power and control of sin. Our "old man" or "old self" in Romans 6:6 refers to our former life in Adam as a slave of sin (Rom. 6:17). Through Christ's death our old life as a slave of sin came to an end so that sin's control over our body has been done away with and we no longer have to serve sin (Rom 6:6)!

It is through Christ's death that a believer has "died to sin". (Rom. 6:2) "Death" in Scripture always speaks of some kind of separation. Physical death is the separation of the soul from the body; spiritual death is the separation of a person's life from God; and eternal death is the separation of a person's life from God forever. Death to sin speaks of being separated from the rule or reign of sin and now living under the rule and reign of Christ's grace (cf. Rom 5:21).

The Spirit of God has baptized or united every Christian into not only His death but also His resurrection. The practical effect of this is clearly revealed. One can now live a new life of victory over sin (Rom. 6:4).

When I finished high school I joined the Air Force and on a hot July day flew to San Antonio, Texas to do my basic training. A bus met the recruits at the airport and took us to

Lackland Air Force Base. The first person we met on the base was our sergeant. It did not take long to discover who would be the boss over the next six weeks. His word was final and his orders were to be obeyed implicitly.

What would it be like if I met my old sergeant some thirty plus years later. If he started barking orders at me, I might instinctively respond at first. However, it would not take me too long to realize that I have a new relationship to the sergeant, and I do not have to obey his orders!

Sin will still try to bark its orders at you and attempt to defeat your efforts to pray and obey God. You do not have to respond; you are "in Christ". His death and resurrection has had a practical effect on your life. His death has liberated you from sin's rule and His resurrection enables you to live a new life! Only when you live and pray from this foundation will you experience the victory that Christ died and rose again to give you. Believe God to practically teach you all that it means to be "in Christ," and ask Him for the grace to introduce others to this liberating truth.

CHAPTER FOURTEEN

SEEING YOURSELF FOR WHO YOU REALLY ARE AS YOU PRAY

Jaime Escalante told a story about a fellow high school teacher who one year had two students in his class named "Johnny". One was a model student and the other Johnny was the other extreme and expended little effort in his studies. At the first PTA meeting of the year, a mother approached the teacher and asked, "How is my son, Johnny, getting along?" Assuming her to be the mother of the model student, he replied, "I can't tell you how much I enjoy him. I'm so glad he's in my class."

The following day the problem Johnny came up to his teacher and said, "My mom told me what you said last night. I haven't ever had a teacher who wanted me in his class." After doing all his assignments, he turned in his completed homework the next day. Within a few weeks this "lazy" student became a hard-working student. His life was turned around because he sensed he was no longer perceived as a problem student.

In my own personal experience my fourth grade teacher had a pivotal impact upon my academic life. In good-natured fun my older brother was kidding me with such statements as, "You should consider taking some IQ tests because I'm not sure you have all your marbles." The only problem with this kidding is that he had no idea I was taking him so seriously. I could also hear the words of my second grade teacher reverberating through my mind. One afternoon after recess this beautiful lady stormed into class, and all I remember are the words, "I bet that Bill Thrasher did that." I had not done anything at that time but it certainly reinforced in my mind that she perceived me as a problem.

Into this picture entered my fourth grade teacher, Mrs. Peterson, who believed in me and convinced me that I could make all "A's". She transformed my young academic life! She won my heart and I owe a great debt to her for giving me a positive vision for my future schooling.

God desires every genuine Christian to know the truth about himself. When one trusts Christ, his bondage and slavery to his self-will (sin) has come to end. He can now live a new life. We **know** this truth the same way we **know** John 3:16: God reveals it in His Word. Christ died to give us freedom from both the guilt and control of sin.

The first command in the book of Romans is Romans 6:11. We are told to view ourselves as a winner in the spiritual realm. Thank Him for the victorious life and ministry that He died to give you. We are dead or separated from sin's control and alive to **Christ**! God asks us to adopt this continual attitude of faith. It is based on Christ's accomplishment, and we are to view ourselves this way regardless of our emotions or past experience. We may not feel like a winner in the spiritual realm and in our experience, we may have known more spiritual defeats than victories in our life. This does not negate the truth that we are placed in a position of victory and are now slaves of righteousness rather than a slave of sin (Rom. 6:18). We are to have the faith of Abraham. It did not seem reasonable to him that under his circumstances he could ever have children. However, he believed God's promise, and God worked miraculously in **His** timing (Rom. 4:19-21). This is what God desires for you.

Listen to another familiar story that I received in an email one day; it is a fitting conclusion to this chapter:

> As she stood in front of her fifth- grade class on the very first day of school, she told the children an untruth. Like most teachers, she looked at her students and said that she loved them all the same, however, that was impossible because there in the front row, slumped in his seat, was a little boy named Teddy Stoddard. Mrs. Thompson had watched Teddy and noticed that he did not play well with the other children, that his clothes were messy, and   that he constantly needed a bath. In addition, Teddy could be unpleasant. It got to the point where Mrs. Thompson would actually take delight in marking his papers with a broad, red pen, making bold red X's and then putting a big "F" at the top of his paper.
>
> At the school where Mrs. Thompson taught, she was required to review each child's past records, and she put Teddy's off until last. However, she was surprised upon reviewing his file. Teddy's first-grade teacher wrote, "Teddy is a bright smile with a ready laugh. He does his

work neatly and has good manners...he is a joy to be around." His second-grade teacher wrote, "Teddy is an excellent student, well liked by his classmates, but he is troubled because his mother has a terminal illness and life at home must be a struggle." His third- grade teacher wrote, "His mother's death has been hard on him. He tries to do his best, but his father doesn't show much interest, and his home life will soon affect him if some steps aren't taken." Teddy's fourth-grade teacher wrote, "Teddy is withdrawn and doesn't show much interest in school. He doesn't have many friends, and he sometimes sleeps in class."

By now, Mrs. Thompson realized the problem and she was ashamed of herself. She even felt worse when her students brought her Christmas presents wrapped in beautiful ribbons and bright paper, except for Teddy's. His present was clumsily wrapped in the heavy, brown paper that he got from a grocery bag. Mrs. Thompson took pains to open it in the middle of the other presents. Some of the children started to laugh when she found a rhinestone bracelet with some of the stones missing, and a bottle that was one-quarter full of perfume. But she stifled the children's laughter when she exclaimed how pretty the bracelet was, putting it on, and dabbing some of the perfume on her wrist. Teddy stayed after school that day just long enough to say, "Mrs. Thompson, today you smelled just like my mom used to."

After the children left, she cried for at least an hour. On that very day she quit teaching reading, writing, and arithmetic. Instead she began to teach children. Mrs. Thompson paid particular attention to Teddy. As she worked with him, his mind seemed to come alive. The more she encouraged him, the faster he responded. By the end of the year, Teddy had become one of the smartest children in the class and, despite her lie that she would love all the children the same, Teddy became one of her, "Teacher's Pets."

A year later, she found a note under her door, from Teddy, telling her that she was the best teacher he had ever had in his whole life. Six years went by before she got another note from Teddy. He then wrote that he had finished High School, third in his class, and she was still the best teacher he had ever had in life. Four years after that, she got another letter saying that while things had been tough at times, he had stayed in school, had stuck with it, and would soon graduate from college with the highest of honors. He assured Mrs. Thompson that she was still the best and favorite teacher he had ever had in his whole life. Then four years passed and yet another letter came. This time he explained that after he had gotten his bachelor's degree he dicied to go a little further. His letter explained that she was still the best and favorite teacher that he had ever had. But now his name was a little longer. The letter was signed, Theodore F. Stoddard, MD.

The story does not end there. You see, there was yet another letter that spring. Teddy said that he had met this girl and he was going to be married. He explained that his father had died a couple of years ago, and he was wondering if Mrs. Thompson might agree to sit at the wedding in the place that was usually reserved for the mother of the groom. Of course, Mrs. Thompson did. And guess what? She wore that bracelet, the one with several rhinestones missing. Moreover, she made sure she was wearing the perfume that Teddy remembered his mother wearing on their last Christmas together. They hugged each other, and Dr. Stoddard whispered in Mrs. Thompson's ear, "Thank you Mrs. Thompson, for believing in me. Thank you so much for making me feel important and showing me that I could make a difference."

Whether this touching story is truth or fiction, it illustrates an important spiritual truth. When you allow the truth of what Jesus thinks of you to sink into your spirit, then and only then can you truly experience the hope that is found in Christ.   Why not let God fill you to the point of overflowing with this hope, in order that others, too, may benefit (Romans 15:13)?

CHAPTER FIFTEEN

PRAYING IN LIGHT OF YOUR FREEDOM

David Seamands tells the story about a covey of quail that a farmer in India brought to the bazaar to sell. After tying a string around one foot of each quail, he tied the other ends of all the strings to a single ring on a stick in the middle of the birds. The result was a covey of quail that continually walked in a circle around the stick. One day a devout Brahman who had a heart of compassion for the pathetic lot of these birds, went to the merchant and expressed his desire to purchase all of them. Of course the merchant was delighted but also surprised when the man insisted that all the strings be cut and the quail be set free. After freeing them they continued marching in a circle continually. Even when he had shooed them away they gathered together a distance away and resumed their marching in a circle. They were free but continued to live as though they were bound!

The believer in Christ does not beg or plead with God to be set free but rather praises God that He is free! This is counting, reckoning or considering oneself to be dead to sin's control and alive to Christ. It is accepting God's truth regardless of our emotions or past experience. Think of your greatest struggle and begin praising God that Christ died and rose again to enable you to honor and obey Him in this struggle. Thank Him that He will guide you into the experience that Christ has purchased for you for His glory.

Ted Engstrom in his helpful book *The Pursuit of Excellence* tells the story of an American Indian who placed an eagle's egg into the nest of a prairie chicken:

> The eagle hatched and grew up with the chicks. All his life the eagle acted like a prairie chicken because he thought he was one. He even sounded like a prairie chicken and only flew a few feet off the ground just like a prairie chicken was supposed to fly.
>
> As the years passed and the eagle grew very old, he saw a majestic bird soaring in the sky far above him hardly even moving its strong golden wings.
>
> "What a beautiful bird!" said the eagle to his neighbor. "What is it?"
>
> "That's an eagle—the chief of birds," the neighbor clucked. "But don't give it a second thought. You could never be like him."

So the eagle never thought about it again and went on living like a prairie chicken. What a tragedy to be **created** to live one way and conditioned to live another way! He was designed to be the chief of all fowl but instead believed the counsel of his neighbor, "You are only a prairie chicken."

When God commands Christians to count, consider, and reckon themselves dead to sin and alive to God in Romans 6:11, he is simply telling us to adopt an attitude of faith about ourselves. He is saying, "Consider yourself to be an eagle and not a prairie chicken because that is really what you are!" Why not right now in the authority of Christ praise God for who you are and ask Him to show you any thoughts in your mind that need to be rejected in order to be filled with His liberating truth to enter into the hope that is in Christ.

CHAPTER SIXTEEN

CRYING OUT TO GOD FOR DELIVERANCE FROM THE DECEIT OF SIN

Warren Weirsbe told about a clever way people in North Africa have devised to catch monkeys. First of all they find a gourd and then make a hole in the gourd that is just large enough for the monkey to stick his hand into it. Afterwards they place nuts into the gourd and tie the gourd to a tree. When the monkey discovers the gourd, he reaches into it and finds the nuts. With his hand full of nuts, the hole is not large enough for him to withdraw his paw. All he has to do is to drop the nuts, and he could escape with no problem. Because he refuses to release his grip on the nuts he gets captured. Could the same thing happen to a person (made in the image of God) who has been freed by Christ?

One has to release his grip on anything that is causing him to sin if he desires to experience true freedom. One cannot play with sin and have victory over it. The loving command by God is to not let the dethroned king (sin) reign again in your body (Rom. 6:12). We are commanded to not present the members of our body to sin as instruments of unrighteousness (Rom. 6:13). Jesus shed his blood to allow you to be a winner in these battles. In fact you are winner, and winning is obeying God and experiencing continual, meaningful fellowship with Him in prayer!

Suppose you discovered a burglar attempting to break into your place of residence one evening. Upon inquiring about his activity, he plainly tells you that he is trying to break into your home and rob you. Is it likely that you would aid him in his activity? Would you say, "You certainly are having a difficult time, but wait here a minute and let me get something for you. Here is a hammer and a crowbar. Perhaps these will assist you." Such a scenario is unthinkable!

When sin comes knocking at the door of your mind, its deceit hides the truth that it is a thief. In fact sin is so deceitful that every believer needs daily encouragement in order to not be **hardened** by sin's deceit (Heb. 3:13). God's commandments are designed for man's **good** and to sin against His wise ways is to **injure oneself**.

> And to keep the LORD'S commandments and His statutes which I am commanding you today for your good. (Deut. 10:13, emphasis added)

> "But he who sins against me injures himself;
> All those who hate me love death." (Prov. 8:36, emphasis added)

Perhaps we talk too little of the destructive nature of sin. Would not Samson's desire for Delilah have been different if he could also have envisioned his eyes gouged out and his humiliation by the Philistines? Would not have Bathsheba appeared different if David could have foreseen the great devastation the brief pleasure would bring upon the future generations of his family?

Sin is a **thief** according to Jeremiah 5:25. Sin results in a loss of true joy, fellowship with God, the full **experience** of God's love, confidence, spiritual power, and spiritual insight. It hinders our relationship with others and results in the loss of eternal reward for a believer and the experience of an eternal hell for an unbeliever. It you are a Christian sin will not condemn you; however, it will rob you!

One of the greatest evidence of God's power is His gracious conviction of sin that enables us to see the deceitful and destructive nature of sin. During his reign the Roman emperor Diocletian unleashed great persecution against the church. In August of 303 A.D. the emperor attended a play in Rome. The play was designed to make fun of the Christians. Gesenius one of the actors dressed in white fell to the floor and in a joking way expressed his faith in Christ and his desire to be a martyr for his Lord. As the crowd laughed at this fake baptism, Gesenius, who was raised in a Christian home, felt pangs of conviction. The conviction was so strong that he cried out, "I want to receive the grace of Christ that I might be born again and be set free from the sins that have been my ruin." Because he realized the audience felt he was still acting, he said, "Illustrious emperor and all the people who have laughed loudly at this parody, believe me! Christ is the true Lord!"

The enraged emperor ordered Genesius to be tortured at once. He stayed firm in his worship of Christ whom he declared to be his only King and his willingness to die a thousand deaths. Would you respond to the loving conviction of God who desires to set you free from the deceitfulness of sin and to experience your victory in Christ?   In the authority of Christ, cry out to Christ to deliver you and your loved ones from the deceit of sin.

CHAPTER SEVENTEEN

LIVING AND PRAYING WITH RESURRECTION POWER

If one could read the hearts of thousands who attend church week after week, would it be discovered that many have "given up" inside, concerning some battles in their lives? Why is there an epidemic of half-hearted living and praying in the pews? The honest response of many might be, "Why be whole-hearted about something that you are not sure really works?" The truth is that many professing Christians do not believe that prayer really makes any difference. Furthermore, they do not believe the preacher thinks it does either; they just think that he has to say so in order to not be fired.

Understanding the practical significance of our union with Christ should drive out a sense of hopelessness, helplessness, and pessimism, and replace it with a vivid hope. The starting point of accepting this is to think of your greatest struggle and begin praising God that Christ died and rose again to give you victory in this specific area.

Praise Him that He will train you to experience the victory that Christ purchased for you for His glory!

Perhaps your struggle is a relational struggle. Every time a certain person acts in a certain way, they push your button and you respond wrongly. You may feel as if your only hope is to somehow avoid them. Jesus died to deliver you from this wrong response and rose again to empower you to build a new response of discerning love. In Christ you have a dynamic **beyond** yourself to sustain the relationships of your life!

Some use the term "stronghold" to speak of a particular bondage in one's life when there is a repeated yielding to the flesh in disobedience to God. Jesus died to give us "hope" in these sinful responses that we have allowed to be programmed into our lives. Jesus shed His blood not only to forgive you but also to give you the authority to build a new, godly response to replace the sinful bondage.

After one honestly confesses this sin, he should commit this battle to the Lord, with an openness to Him to do anything He would require. It is also important to look for the "root" of the wrong response and not just treat the symptom. In my first year of teaching I had a student in my class who procrastinated in turning in every assignment. It was, however, the most unusual form of procrastination I have ever seen. He had the papers done on time but would not turn them in on time. Procrastination was not his root problem. It was **fear**! All of his life he felt that whatever he did was not good enough. He later told me how much courage it took to hand his papers to me and give someone else an opportunity to criticize his work! Actually his work was quite well done, and he made progress as he faced his fear.

Christ died and rose again to set you free to love and obey Him. When we unwisely sin as believers, we are living inconsistently with our true identity as a "slave of righteousness" (Rom. 6:18). Our response to sin should be to agree with God's conviction and accept His faithful cleansing (1 John 1:9). I have also found it very helpful to praise God that I am no longer a slave to the sin which I have committed. This is once again entering into the truth of Romans 6:11. Furthermore, I present to the Lord once again whatever part of my body was involved in the sin so as to make even this moment one of consecration to God (Rom. 6:12-13). I pray that you can experience this victorious response to your failures and introduce this response to countless others!

A dear friend shared with me one day a deep struggle in his soul. We met later that week, and I shared with him for the greater part of a day many of the insights that had been a help to me in temptation. We concluded our time together on our knees in prayer. As he prayed for the struggle we had discussed, he uttered a feeble, "Please help me." I said, "Stop! You are not praying in light of the victory Christ purchased for you." He agreed and we continued praying. As he drove away I decided to walk down the street to a restaurant to get something to eat. On the way to the restaurant I had an intense prayer burden for my friend. All I could think of were some of the prayers of Ephesians 1:15-23. I prayed, "Lord give him **hope**; Lord give him **power**." For thirty minutes I prayed until the prayer burden lifted. I gave up on the idea of eating and returned to my apartment. When I called my friend the next day and told him of the prayer burden, he began to chuckle. He told me that at that exact time the Lord began to uncover the sense of despair he had in this area of his life. He pulled a book off his shelf dealing with spiritual warfare and began to pray in the authority of Jesus. This was the beginning of the process of God implanting hope in his life and uprooting the devilish sense of despair.

God desires to do the same for you and me. Resurrection power is the power that can give victory out of apparent defeat. When Jesus was in the grave, it looked as if the enemies of unrighteousness were winning. However, the Lord was defeating evil and afterwards came the resurrection. In your struggle God desires to give you "hope" and allow you to experience His resurrection power. It may take time to fully experience this victory but praise Jesus that the victory is yours (cf. Exod. 23:29-30). It is something that He not only wants you to experience, but He wants you to experience it so profoundly that many others will experience it also, through what He has graciously done for and through you.

CHAPTER EIGHTEEN

REALIZING GOD'S LOVING PROVISIONS

Victorious Christian living and prayer is always undergirded by an attitude of self-surrender. God's loving provision and exhortation to enable one to present himself and every part of his body to His control is preceded by the revelation of His unconditional love and delight in His people (Rom. 5:1-8 precedes Rom. 6:12-13 and 12:1-2). Even in the midst of your struggle with sin there is Someone who loves you and cares for you. When you go through hurtful situations and you do not receive the understanding or the appreciation and love you need, you can rest in God's continual love and delight in you. As the Lord allows things in your life to reveal your insufficiency, these are designed to result in a deeper experience of God's incredible love and power.

One does not need to "do anything" to make himself acceptable to God--not even pray. Christ has done it all. One does not present his life to Christ in order to gain His acceptance but rather in light of His acceptance. When one is resting in God's love he is released from the need to impress others. The love He has for you is a love that you have never experienced from anyone else on this earth in exactly the same way. Despite knowing everything about you—even every thought that has ever gone through your mind, He loves you and yearns- to have an intimate relationship with you!

God **demonstrated** this love by sending His Son to walk on this earth and live a perfect life of love and sacrificially die for you. He gave you a written record of His loving revelation to you and His Spirit to make this revelation real and personal to you. He wants you to live knowing His gracious smile upon your life. When the Spirit of God has the freedom in a community of believers to witness the reality of this, God's people are set free, and they are able to achieve things they never thought possible.

As one sees the truth of God's character and what He has done, the exhortation to present oneself to Him makes sense. In fact, if there is a Person who is perfectly wise, loving, and righteous, and it is possible to put ourselves under His control, would it not be insane not to do so? Sin is insane and the world promotes this insanity by encouraging dependent creatures to live independently of God. If you saw a thousand light bulbs in your life and nine hundred and ninety of them were lying on the floor and only ten were screwed into sockets giving light, you might think that that which is abnormal is normal. That is the pressure of the world that wars against God's design for man to abide in Him.

Many "successful" people are inwardly quite bored. Why? They may have a prestigious job, but there is a boredom factor in their life. Let's say that one's work requires sixty percent of his total abilities to do his job. He has a forty percent boredom factor. In God's great love He made it possible for a believer in Christ to present the totality of his life to the Lord. In the words of Romans 6:13 all the members of your body can become "instruments of righteousness." In this sense one may have a job that does not require all of his abilities but his whole being is involved in "life" because every part of himself is available and in fellowship with God as he experiences the grace to abide in Him.

Never underestimate what God can accomplish through even one life which has been truly presented to God. It was D.L. Moody who was challenged by the words, "It remains for the world to see what the Lord can do with a man wholly consecrated to Christ." His response was, "Lord make me that man!" The impact of his response is revealed in his forty years of ministry and its lasting influence.

Telemachs was a fourth century Christian whose boldness Charles Colson recounts in his excellent book *Loving God*. Living in a remote village he invested most of his time in prayer and tending his garden. Thinking he heard the voice of God instructing him to go to Rome, he set forth on foot and arrived weeks later at the time of a great festival. Following the crowd to the coliseum, he saw the gladiators offering themselves up to die to entertain the crowd. He cried out, "In the name of Christ, stop!"

Pushing himself through the crowd and climbing over the wall, he entered the arena and continued to shout, "In the name of Christ, stop!" The crowd laughed at the little man thinking that he was part of the show. This laughter quickly turned to anger as he continued to plead with the gladiators to stop the bloodthirsty show. One of them suddenly plunged his sword through Telemachs' body only to hear his dying words, "In the name of Christ, stop!"

A strange thing happened next. The gladiators looked at the tiny dead man and a hush filled the coliseum. Suddenly a man in the upper row made his way to the exit and others began to follow. Everyone eventually left the coliseum in silence.

That fatal day in A.D. 391, was the last time gladiators battled to death in the Roman coliseum for the entertainment of the crowd. One tiny voice in the midst of a loud coliseum made the difference, "One voice—one life that spoke the truth in God's name." There is great fruit when we allow the Lord to set us free to experience the grace of prayer and obey God's promptings.

SECTION THREE

Need for Motivation and Enablement—Experiencing the Grace of Motivation and Enablement

Many people want the right thing but lack the lasting motivation and endurance to achieve it. This section will introduce you to the grace of motivation and enablement that can only be found in Christ. It is my testimony that it is this grace alone that has motivated and sustained me for the last forty years of serving Christ. This grace is the very essence of the Christian life.

God's grace is not only the basis for our initial salvation but also the key to the Christian life from beginning to end. It is not to be known by us merely as a "buzz-word" but as a daily reality that enables us to obey God and keep going in our darkest moments--even when we do not feel like it. May God use you to help others to understand and experience this grace in their lives.

The wonder of being introduced to the reality of the Holy Spirit is something that I have never forgotten. This is something that God not only wants you to progressively experience, but also to be an instrument for sharing this with many others. Why not believe God right now to teach you in such a way that your life could overflow and illustrate to others the Spirit-filled and Spirit-led life. Such a decision of faith on your part will be the cause of much rejoicing from others who will benefit both in time and in eternity!

CHAPTER NINETEEN

UNDERSTANDING GOD'S GRACIOUS MOTIVATION AND ENABLEMENT

One day as I was reading 1 Peter 5, the Spirit of God illuminated the truth of verse two to my heart in a practical way. It was the phrase, "not under compulsion, but voluntarily according to the will of God." In other words we are told that we are not to do God's work because "we have to" but because "we want to!!" This verse does not mean that doing God's will is always accompanied by the same emotions as if we were eating ice cream and pizza, but it does mean that it is not to be an oppressive burden to the believer who is surrendered to God.

One of the most glorious truths in which a believer can rest is that God will provide the motivation and enablement to do anything He requires them to do. If God only gave us commands and not the motivation and enablement to obey them, how could we love such a God from our heart? His commands are designed for our eternal best. Every negative command or prohibition is designed for our protection. Every positive command is His finger pointing to the best and safest path of life. To sin against Him is to also injure oneself (Deut. 10:13; Prov. 8:35-36). When one begins to obey God's truth and pray from the heart, he begins to truly **know** God (1 John 2:5).

This glorious provision is the theme of the apostle Paul's testimony in 1 Corinthians 15. Not only does He credit God's grace with his changed life but also as the key to his Christian **labor**! If you were to ask the apostle Paul, "Did you feel like praying every day?" or even, "Did you feel like getting out of bed every day?"--what do you think he would say? I am sure he would tell you that he did **not** but that he took steps of faith knowing that God's grace would meet him at each demand.

God's grace was not an abstract concept to the apostle as it related to the Christian **life**. It was termed "grace" because it was a divine force that he did not deserve. It referred to the gracious provision of the Spirit to both motivate and enable all of Paul's labor (1 Cor. 15:10; cf. Phil. 2:13). It is the outworking of the New Covenant promise originally given to Israel. The New Testament makes it clear that we share in this new covenant. The promise, "I will put my Spirit within you and **cause** you to walk in my statutes, and you will be careful to observe my ordinances" is the content of what Paul calls the **grace** of His labor in 1 Corinthians 15:10 (cf. Ezek. 36:27).

For this reason, Paul exhorts Timothy to be strengthened by God's **grace** (2 Tim. 2:1). While Timothy did not feel fully adequate for his enormous task in Ephesus, he could experience the adequacy of God. Such is the testimony of Paul in 2 Corinthians 3:5-6 as it relates to the new covenant and the provisions of the Spirit:

> Not that we are adequate in ourselves to consider anything as coming from ourselves, but our adequacy is from God, who also made us adequate as servants of a new covenant, not of the letter but of the Spirit; for the letter kills, but the Spirit gives life. (2 Cor. 3:5-6)

In fact, in all of Paul's letters he almost always begins with the phrase "grace and peace to you". This is not only a greeting but also a prayer that the believers would experience God's grace and peace. While a true believer has already experienced the grace of God that leads to salvation (Eph. 2:8-9), he is in continual need of God's gracious provision to live the Christian life (1 Cor. 15:10). In the same way, while a true believer has peace **with** God (Rom. 5:1), he is in need of the peace **of** God which is conditional upon our casting all our cares upon God (Phil. 4:6-7; 1 Pet. 5:7).

God can be trusted to **always** provide the motivation and enablement we need to do anything He requires us to do. Our responsibility is to "abide" in Him. Just as a plant draws from the soil all it needs to sustain, support, and nourish itself; and a fish draws all it needs from the water; a believer is to totally depend upon Christ. **He** is the vine, and we are the branches. When we confuse our roles and attempt to be the vine, we will fail to benefit from the gracious promises and support of God!

I received an invitation to speak at a Virginia church retreat in the Washington D.C. area. While they graciously offered to fly me and my wife to the retreat, they also gave the alternative of allowing me to drive my whole family and placing us in a Washington D.C. motel for a few days before my speaking began. As I set out to drive on the Monday **after** September 11, 2001, I was so grateful! Of course no plane flights were available in light of the recent national crisis. It was also an unforgettable week for my family to visit Washington D.C. in this critical time in the life our nation.

That retreat enabled me to renew the relationship with Steve King, who was a Campus Crusade for Christ staff member for two years at Auburn University, and had personally discipled me. He was now pastoring Cherrydale Baptist Church in Arlington, Virginia, which had contacted me to do the retreat. We had planned a supper together that would enable us to see each other for the first time in twenty-eight years.

What would it be like to see someone whom I had not seen for almost three decades? I was amazed that he seemed to have hardly changed physically! Even more importantly, the same gracious and encouraging mannerisms that had characterized his ministry at the college I attended were also evident that night at the dinner table! He exhibited the same zeal to be used of God and was as much in love with his wife as when she was his fiancée in his years at Auburn. What a thrill to my soul to see God's grace in this man, this marriage, and this ministry.

One day almost thirty years ago, I contemplated how I could stay true to God for the next forty or fifty years if I were to live a normal life. As I entertained this thought for only about a minute, I became exhausted. Then God brought to my mind the truth of Philippians 2:13:

> For it is God who is at work in you, both to will and to work for His good pleasure. (Phil. 2:13)

What brought peace to my heart was that there would never be a day that God would not be with me: motivating and enabling me to do His will and graciously convicting me of my sin. *He* would keep me going—one day at a time— one moment at a time.

Romans 15:5 is the verse that gave me the courage to get out of bed each day one difficult summer. I saw that God is the One who gives encouragement and *endurance!* Each day I would write down how God kept me going. In God's unchanging faithfulness He will do it every day. His mercies are new *every* morning. Great is His faithfulness (Lam. 3:23)! We can say:

Yesterday God helped me.

Today He will do the same.

How long will it last? Forever.

Praise His name.

Look to God as the only *Source* for everything you need. Spend time praising and thanking Him that He will give you the daily grace to pray and live for Him. If we meet twenty-eight years from now, may our experience be such that we are still ministering and crying out in prayer to this faithful God.

CHAPTER TWENTY

LABORING AND PRAYING IN GOD'S GRACE

What is the secret to being able to genuinely love? Only Jesus' love can call Judas "friend", pray for those who crucified Him, and accept Saul of Tarsus and make him an apostle. Unless one learns to labor in the Lord, our labor is truly in vain:

> Unless the LORD builds the house,
> They labor in vain who build it;
> Unless the LORD guards the city,
> The watchman keeps awake in vain. (Ps. 127:1)

In the Christian life we are always trying to figure out "What is our part?" and "What is God's part?" One day we are exhorted to discipline ourselves and buffet our bodies (1 Cor. 9:27); the next day we are told that we are trying too hard and need to "let go and let God." Who is right? I think Colossians 1:29 gives us the balance:

> For this purpose also I labor, striving according to His power which mightily works within me. (Col. 1:29)

The Christian life is a *labor*, but it is a labor empowered by God. There is a difference between simply laboring and striving, and laboring and striving in God's strength. Both can tire you out, but one does so much sooner. One leaves you inwardly refreshed and the other inwardly exhausted. One is a labor of faith with the burden of the labor cast upon God, and the other is a labor of self-effort with the burden of the work upon our shoulders. Armin Gesswien said that laboring is drudgery; laboring for the Lord is dreary, but laboring with the Lord is delight.

The apostle Paul tells us that the secret to his labor was God's grace:

> But by the grace of God I am what I am, and His grace toward me did not prove vain; but I labored even more than all of them, yet not I, but the grace of God with me. (1 Cor. 15:10)

He meant that the Lord provided the motivation and power for all that He called him to do. It is this same grace that he recommended to Timothy, "Be strong in grace" (2 Tim. 2:1), and to every believer, as he starts his epistles with the phrase "grace and peace."

This "grace" is the secret of every facet of Christian service and the key to prayer. God gives the grace of prayer as well as the grace of study, the grace to respond properly to a trial, or in other words, the grace to do *anything* He commands us to do. In this sense, every command contains a hidden promise. He will not command you to do anything that He will not motivate and empower His children to do, as you humble yourself to receive this grace. All of our challenges and inadequacies are to draw us to His resources. He has commanded us to pray without ceasing, and He will give us the grace to do so!

For example, 2 Corinthians 8 and 9 speak of the grace of giving. This grace was given to the churches of Macedonia (2 Cor. 8:1), and their giving is referred to as a *gracious* work. As a high school boy I would occasionally place a dollar bill in the offering plate. A friend next to me would whisper in my ear, "That is one less dollar you have for the car you plan to buy." The sad thing is, that is exactly how I looked at it. This is not the grace of giving!

Immediately after college and before seminary, I worked for a summer at a church in Chattanooga, Tennessee. A dear family graciously allowed me to live with them so that my expenses were next to nothing. I was paid one hundred dollars a week for the ten weeks of my summer ministry and was given the one thousand dollar check during my first week. That same summer there was a very significant Christian conference being held in Korea. God gave me a great burden for it and the thought that began to grip my mind was to give the one thousand dollars to this conference. After wrestling with this, I, who had never been able to give a dollar, gave the one thousand dollars. It is not that I am necessarily a great giver today, but I do know that God gives grace in this area. The question is: How are you and I responding to this grace today?

In my book, *A Journey to Victorious Praying,* [17] I state how after a number of years of giving myself to the discipline of prayer, I began to drown in the growing number of prayer requests that inundated my life. I would not have felt this way had I understood the truth of this chapter. I discovered that although I continued to pray, I did not really expect God to do anything. When we pray with no expectancy, our prayer life has died. The concept of the grace of prayer resurrected my dead prayer life. Has your prayer life died? Why not cry out to God to illuminate your mind to understand His grace and revive your prayer life?

Joe Bayly told a story that Billy Graham related to some missionaries who had just lost everything during a political uprising in their African country. He told how a very wealthy man was sharing with a small church why God had blessed him with his millions and millions of dollars. He said, "It all started when as a young man; I had a dollar in one pocket and a quarter in the other." As the offering plate came around he talked to himself, "Will I give the dollar or the quarter, the dollar or the quarter, the dollar or the quarter?" When the offering plate came to him, he said, "I gave both the quarter and the dollar. I gave it all and that is why God has blessed me." A little lady from the back of the church said, "I dare him to do it again!" Would he now give

[17] Bill Thrasher, *A Journey to Victorious Praying* (Chicago, Moody Press 2003).

his millions? Billy Graham reminded these missionaries that when they came to the field, they gave it all. Now that they had lost everything, they were being encouraged to do it again. As you and I give ourselves to the Lord we can learn to labor and pray in God's grace.

CHAPTER TWENTY-ONE

WALKING BY THE SPIRIT IN ALL OF LIFE

If one looks at prayer or ministry as only an isolated Christian activity, he will not experience the grace of prayer and ministry. It is an overflow of a life that walks by the Spirit. As a nineteen- year-old college student, I wandered into the room of a fraternity brother at Auburn University. This dedicated Christian young man began to talk to me about the Holy Spirit. I did not respond in any way that November day over thirty years ago. I did leave with the thought, "Maybe there is hope in living the Christian life." While I did acknowledge Christ as my Savior and outwardly my life was enjoying success in college, inwardly I was full of fear and anxiety. I followed up with this visit by reading a book over Christmas break on the Holy Spirit and a plan to room with this fraternity brother the next year. That year transformed my life.

The Holy Spirit is a *Person*. He is also *God* as the eternal and coequal third Person in the Trinity. Before the Lord Jesus left the earth and ascended into heaven, He promised to not leave His disciples as orphans. He would send them the Spirit whom He called the "Helper". When one becomes a Christian, he has a Person who lives in him and goes with him everywhere he goes! This *Person* is *God* the Holy Spirit, and we need to learn to lean on His Divine *Help* for everything we do. This is called *walking* by the Spirit (Gal. 5:16).

Why do we need the Holy Spirit? First of all, we have spiritual enemies that are too big for us *but* no match for the resources of God. We need to continually lean on the promise that "Greater is He who is in you than he who is in the world" (1 John 4:4). Secondly, the life that God calls us to live is beyond what we can live in our own strength. To love each other as Christ loved us requires the help of the Holy Spirit to produce His fruit of love in us (John 13:34; Gal. 5:22). The Holy Spirit is God's gracious provision because He provides the motivation and enablement to live the Christian life and to pray.

In Chapter Nineteen, we noted that if God only gave us His kind commands and not the grace to live them out, we could not love Him with all our hearts. It is for this reason that when elders are instructed concerning shepherding the flock of God, they are told to do it "not under compulsion, but *voluntarily*" (1 Peter 5:2, emphasis added). It is this "want to" motivation and inward drive that Paul refers to as "grace" in the Christian life. He talked about it in his own experience (1 Cor. 15:10) and in the experiences of others (2 Cor. 8:3-5). It is what he desired Philemon to appropriate in forgiving Onesimus who had stolen from him and run away. He did not simply desire to *order*

Philemon to do the right thing (Philemon 8) but rather to appeal to him so that his kindness would not be something Paul forced on him but what truly sprung from his own desired choice (Philemon 14). It is the will of God that you experience this in your ministry and life today. Here is how:

It Requires an Openness to God's Control

Is there any area of your life that is not open to the Lord's control? If you are a Christian you already have all of the Spirit, but the question is whether or not He has all of you. Fear is often what hinders our openness to God's control. Seek God at your point of fear and open your life to His love that can cast out your fear and transform it into faith. Remember courage is simply fear that has said its prayers.

It Requires a Dependence Upon God's Control

Over thirty years ago Howard Hendricks told me that when he became a Christian he wrote these words in his Bible: "When I try I fail; when I trust He succeeds." He then said it has taken all of his Christian life to truly discern the meaning of these words.

A number of years ago, I was reading a book that spoke of three stages of the Christian life. The first was the "I can" stage where we make resolutions and promises to obey God. This is characteristic of many of us who want to pray. Our failure leads to the "I can't" stage because we see the impossibility of maintaining our ministries and prayer lives. The third stage is the "I can't but I must and *God* will enable!" stage. I personally believe that we cycle through three stages as God teaches us a deeper and deeper dependence on Him.

We cannot trust God or depend on Him for any matter that we have not fully surrendered to Him. For this reason Psalm 37:5 tells us to, "Commit [our] way to the Lord, trust also in Him, and He will do it." In prayer I have often asked myself, "What am I involved in, in which I am not following the guidance of Psalm 37:5?" Have I truly committed the task to the Lord? Am I trusting Him alone? As we trust Him, He will show us our responsibility. Dependence on God's control does not always mean inactivity but it does mean activating our faith before we activate our will. I have sometimes discovered that I was trusting in *my effort* to work out a problem or misunderstanding. Such insight required a response of confession and renewed faith in God to work out the situation and waiting on Him for any effort He would have me to do.

It Requires a Responsiveness to God's Control

Responding to the Lord in prayer involves keeping our obedience up to date. Is God prompting you to do something that you are not doing? It also involves confessing our sin. "We are to be as sensitive to sin as the pupils of our eyes are to foreign matter," was the late Dr. Stephen Olford's admonition to God's people.

One of our greatest joys may not be in never falling but in rising every time we fall. As we confess our sin, God is able to cleanse us and fill us afresh with His Spirit:

> For a righteous man falls seven times, and rises again,
> But the wicked stumble in time of calamity. (Prov.
> 24:16)

Why not put your finger on Ephesians 6:18 and Jude 20 and ask God to teach you to pray and minister in the Spirit. He loves you and accepts you and is a patient and gentle teacher. Tell Him not only that you desire to learn this truth, but, in reverence to Him, that you are not willing to live without it! This is the pathway to becoming an effective soul physician.

CHAPTER TWENTY-TWO

GROWING IN GRACE

I remember the counsel of a godly pastor to his dear wife as she was anticipating their fourth child. She stated, "I know God wants us to have this baby, but my life is filled to the brim *now*! How can I possibly care for and nurture another child?" His wise and gentle words were, "When God gave us one child, He gave us one-baby grace. When He gave us two children, He gave us two-baby grace. When He gave us three children, He gave us three-baby grace. God is going to give us something that we have never experienced. He is going to give us four-baby grace."

In 2 Peter 3:18, God commands us to *grow* in the grace and knowledge of the Lord Jesus. In the words of John, the Christian life is characterized by one experience of grace after another:

> For of His fullness we have all received, and grace upon grace. (John 1:16)

The experiences of life are designed to encourage us to come boldly to the throne of grace (Heb. 4:16). What does it mean to come boldly? It means to come with freedom. It involves telling the Lord about our struggles. I was always encouraged by God's command to come boldly to His throne, but my problem was how to come boldly when I had the wrong attitude and I knew I had the wrong attitude. It involves telling the Lord about this wrong attitude! What happens when you do this? According to Hebrews 4:16, you receive merciful understanding and gracious enablement in your struggle! You will not get into trouble if you take your temptations and turn them into honest conversations with God. Such openness will even take some of the deceitful appeal out of the temptation.

Over twenty years ago, I found myself praying to God to bless my relationship with a very godly older man. I struggled as I prayed, because I sensed my request was motivated by a selfish agenda. I continued to struggle in this request until an event occurred one Friday afternoon. A student came to my office and began to verbally abuse me and accuse me because of a misunderstanding. Although he graciously apologized for this the next week, the situation left me humbled as I wrestled with it over the weekend. However, during this weekend I felt my soul being purified, and I sensed the grace to believe God to bless the relationship with the older man I mentioned earlier. God gives grace to the humble and can entrust us with providential circumstances that aid us in humbling ourselves before Him.

God is opposed to the proud, but gives grace to the humble (James 4:6). A point of pride is any area of resistance where our will is set up against His. It is any area of our life where we are not in agreement with Him or any area where we are telling Him, "No." Responding to His gracious conviction (which we will explore in the coming chapter) can enable us to grow in grace

God entrusted Paul with what he called a "thorn in the flesh." While we cannot be certain of the exact nature of the struggle, we do know that it was painful and Paul deeply desired deliverance from it. While Satan desires to use these thorns to destroy us, God desires to use them to humble us and enable us to experience more grace (cf. 2 Cor. 12:7-10)!

The Galatian Christians began the Christian life by faith but were being deluded into trying to continue it by a life of self-effort:

> Are you so foolish? Having begun by the Spirit, are you now being perfected by the flesh? (Gal. 3:3)

It is the will of God that you live in the freedom of this grace that Christ earned for you, minister in this grace, and introduce it to others.

SECTION FOUR

NEED FOR COMFORT IN YOUR PAIN—EXPERIENCING THE GRACE OF PERSPECTIVE THAT OVERCOMES BITTERNESS

When I meet an older believer who has walked with God for many years and is still cheerful, joyful, and free of bitterness; I know that I am observing a walking miracle. To be sure, they have had many opportunities to develop a bitter spirit, but have experienced the grace that has enabled them to choose not to do so.

May the following chapters lead your life and ministry into a fuller experience of this same grace that will work this miracle in and through you. And may God give us the grace to see His kindness in our pain and lead others to do the same.

CHAPTER TWENTY-THREE

TRUSTING THE LORD WITH DIFFICULTY

Although it was many years ago, I will never forget the day I read Psalm 18:19. The last part of the verse says, "He rescued me, because He delighted in me." While I was aware that I was to delight in God (Ps. 37:4) I had never digested the concept that He delighted in me! One day I decided to look up all the references to the Hebrew word, which in this verse is translated delight. One of the references that surprised me was Isaiah 53:10. "But the Lord was pleased [same Hebrew word translated delight] to crush Him, putting Him to grief."

Bruce and Valerie Morrison were a delightful couple who had the burden to make Christ's rest known to the people of mainland China. It was this common ministry burden that drew them together in marriage. They were blessed with six precious girls. In February of 2001, in the midst of their loving, sacrificial service, Bruce was murdered. This left Valerie as a single parent of six daughters, with the oldest being seven years old. She said, "I had rather raise six children with the Lord's help than one child without Him!" As she was visiting in our home a few months after her husband's death, one of the children spontaneously spoke up at the dinner table, "I guess if more people come to know Jesus then it is O.K. if Daddy died, isn't it Mommy?" The four-year-old girl somehow had seen the overwhelming comfort and peace that God had poured out on her family. The circumstances are not what anyone would ask for, but there is the "peace of God that surpasses all comprehension" (Phil. 4:7). Valerie and her six girls returned to China to communicate the love and peace of Jesus to these precious people. She and her girls are actively praying for the man who killed her husband and the murderer's family.

At Moody's Founder's Week Bible Conference in February 2001 I had heard the missionary spokesman Elizabeth Elliot speak and tell the story of her husband's death at the hands of the Indians, that left her widowed with an infant daughter. She shared that the news of Jim's death had fostered in her the thought, "Lord, how can I reach those people who murdered my husband?" I thought, "O God, this is a different Christianity than most of us are experiencing. Would you please raise up more Elizabeth Elliots?" It was a few days after this that I got the call and was informed of the death of Bruce Morrison. In God's kindness He has provided Valerie another husband and a continued ministry in China.

What is the most challenging difficulty with which you need to trust God? Have you been neglected or even rejected and betrayed in an intimate relationship in your life? Have you been treated unfairly or falsely accused? Have you been belittled, insulted, or even abused? Have you been conspired against or controlled and made to feel as if you do not measure up or belong? Have you been made fun of, humiliated, taken advantage of, or publicly shamed? One way to deal with these pains is to attempt to bury them and try to cope with life. However, the lingering unresolved tensions are still there and greatly affect our relationship with God and others.

In the environment of God's grace and in the enablement of His Spirit we need to courageously and prayerfully admit our hurt to God. It may be that God has entrusted you with a very sensitive personality in which you have a deeper capacity to feel emotional pain. It is easy for any of us to wrongly process this pain by responding in unrighteous anger.

In my own life, I knew that God was displeased with my unrighteous anger, and I felt very distant from God in attempting to process the pain myself. However, when I began to see God's interest and desire that in my hurt and pain I come in freedom to Him at His throne of grace, this opened up a new level of intimacy with God. This is the first step in trusting God with your difficulties—a candid, honest, heartfelt talk with Him about the troubles of your soul.

There is One who can identify with you. "Remember Jesus Christ" was Paul's instruction to Timothy (2 Timothy 2:8). Our wonderful Savior suffered for us. He knows what it feels like to be betrayed by a friend (Matt. 26:47-50), and deserted by His followers (Matt. 26:56, 69-75). He knows what it is like to be so grieved that you do not even feel like living any longer (Matt. 26:37-38). He has experienced weariness in His crying and search for comfort only to find none! (Ps. 69:3, 20). He was the object of malicious jealousy and intense hatred by the religious leaders of His day (Matt. 27:18).

There is little more destructive, humiliating, and demeaning to a person than a slap on the face; however, even more humiliating is to be spat on, in the face. This was considered the greatest insult that could be offered to a person (Deut. 25:9, Job 30:10). Jesus was spat on as well as beaten and slapped in the face (Matt. 26:67).

Painful memories of being mocked can drive you to Jesus for comfort knowing that He too was humiliated and made fun of as He approached the cross (Matt. 27:29-30). He was linked with robbers (Matt. 27:38) and He endured unjust accusations during an illegal trial. The physical sufferings of having His head pierced with thorns, His back deeply cut from being beaten by a leather whip that had pieces of bone or metal imbedded in its thongs, and His hands and His feet being torn with iron spikes, were not the greatest aspect of His suffering. It was not even the emotional suffering of being mocked and reviled by His cruel enemies and being deserted by His friends. It was the spiritual suffering of being forsaken by God the Father (Matt. 27:46). He can identify with the great pain of being abandoned and is a wonderful High Priest who can feel with those who have suffered the loss of loved ones through divorce and death. He has endured our hell of being separated from God so that He could give all those who come to Him in repentance and faith, the precious promise, "I will never desert you, nor will I ever forsake you so that we may confidently say, the Lord is my helper, I will not be afraid. What shall man do to me" (Heb. 13:5-6).

Will you, right now talk to the God of grace who will never forsake you? Tell Him how you feel and what you would like Him to do. Do not depend on your feelings to measure His love for you. His love is grounded in His unchanging character as recorded in His Word. His mercies will never come to an end but will be new every morning. Put your trust and hope in Him. God can pour His comfort on you in a way that will not only benefit you but many others as well.

CHAPTER TWENTY-FOUR

GAINING GOD'S PERSPECTIVE TO PROCESS YOUR PAIN THROUGH PRAYER

Perspective is an essential part of responding correctly to trials. In fact, it may be that a lack of perspective is the very essence of the trial. I remember reading the following excerpt one day, which said:

> The greatest tests are those times when people are not at the end of their rope. It takes a real pastor to go into a family where someone has just been promoted to the presidency of the local bank and say, "Mary, I've just gotten the news of your promotion. So I rushed right over knowing this promotion is placing you in an extremely vulnerable position as far as your soul is concerned. I wanted to

come beside you during this time of potential temptation. Could we pray?"[18]

I remember a dear pastor whose incorrect response to a trial in his church had resulted in his having to temporarily leave the ministry. He inappropriately gave them a piece of his mind, which he thought they "deserved." But now he would love to be able to rewind and replay that scenario. He told me, "If only I could have gotten away for awhile and gained perspective, I know I would have responded differently."

George Matheson was born on March 27, 1847, the son of a wealthy Glasgow merchant. He is known and loved by believers all over the world because of the four-verse hymn he wrote—"O Love That Wilt Not Let Me Go." The story attributed to the background of this hymn was Matheson's being rejected by his fiancée when she discovered he was going blind. "I do not want to marry a blind man!" In MacMillan's biography of George Matheson, Matheson describes the circumstances which caused him severe mental suffering. He refers to the hymn as a fruit of his suffering.[19]

An old Puritan writer tells the story of one man who threw a bag of gold to a companion. As the man put his arms out to catch it, the bag hit the man's head and temporarily knocked him out. "What should be the man's response after

---

[18] George Bulnick, *Salt of the Earth*, March/April 1996.

[19] D. MacMillan. *The Life of George Matheson*, (London: Hudder and Stoughton, 1907)

he comes to?" was the writer's point. He will not get up and curse the man for giving him a bag of gold! Trials are like that bag of gold. They may temporarily knock you out but they also enrich your life.

When Mary and Martha cried out for Jesus to help their sick brother, they said, "Lord, behold, he whom You love is sick" (John 11:3). How did Jesus respond to this cry of desperation? Rather than rushing to Lazarus' aid, he stayed two days longer in the place where He was (John 11:6). The short parenthetical comment before the record of our Lord's delayed response speaks volumes. "Now Jesus **loved** Martha, and her sister, and Lazarus (emphasis added)." When our cries for help are met with inexplicable delay, we can rest in Christ's personal love for us. The delay resulted in Lazarus' death. The words of his sister to our Lord at the moment of His arrival were, "Lord, if you had been here, my brother would not have died."

If we only take snapshots of our life on earth, we can get very confused. Most of us do not get upset at the Lord's two-day delay because we know the end of the story-- Lazarus' miraculous resurrection from the dead. To be sure, the only way to be comforted in our pain is to look to the end of the story. On this side of eternity, we cannot answer every question about human tragedies, miscarriages, unjust sufferings, and countless other circumstances. We can, however, refuse to fixate on only one scene of the play and trust God to direct the entire script of our life as we turn our confusion over to our loving Lord. May you envision the truth of Jesus weeping with you in your pain and may His incredible love be manifested to those around you (cf. John

11:35-36). Let the questions of the temporary snapshot lead you to contemplate the end of the story:

> For I consider that the sufferings of this present time are not worthy to be compared with the glory that is to be revealed to us. (Rom. 8:18)

> In this you greatly rejoice, even though now for a little while, if necessary, you have been distressed by various trials, so that the proof of your faith, being more precious than gold which is perishable, even though tested by fire, may be found to result in praise and glory and honor at the revelation of Jesus Christ. (I Pet. 1:6-7)

> For momentary, light affliction is producing for us an eternal weight of glory far beyond all comparison, while we look not at the things which are seen, but at the things which are not seen; for the things which are seen are temporal, but the things which are not seen are eternal. (2 Cor. 4:17-18)

Are we rejoicing in our future hope? Or are too many of us occupied with the things of this world? Seek God through the Scriptures and ask Him to give you a glimpse of all that awaits you. We are told to fix our hope completely on this future grace (1 Pet. 1:13). Write down all the specific things you anticipate experiencing in heaven such as living in a perfect environment of love, enjoying perfect fellowship with Christ and others, free from conflicts and misunderstandings, and being able to perfectly worship and serve Christ. The only thing that made Paul's afflictions appear light (see 2 Cor. 11:16-33) was the vividness of his future hope. How could people have "accepted joyfully the seizure of your property" (Heb. 10:34) unless they were focusing on this future hope?

One day a pitiful leper came to Jesus and begged for His help. Feeling compassion on this despised outcast of society who had no human hope, Christ touched him and spoke one brief phrase, "I am willing, be cleansed" (Mark 1:41). This one touch and this one sentence transformed this man's life forever. While Jesus is no longer walking the face of the earth, He is still living and available as our risen Savior. He can place His compassionate hand on the hurts of your soul and speak His healing words.

His healing is not always instantaneous; more often it is a process. How do you know when you have God's healing hand on the hurts of your soul? It is when you can at least by faith thank Him for the good that He can work out of your pain. This was the faith of Joseph, after being sold and abandoned by his brothers:

> As for you, you meant evil against me, but God meant it for good in order to bring about this present result, to preserve many people alive. (Gen. 50:20)

God is not the blameworthy author of evil, rather, He is sovereign over it and able to work it together for the good of His children (Rom. 8:28). Come boldly to His throne of grace and tell the Lord you desire His healing touch upon the pain of your soul. Tell Him you desire to be touched in a way that will even affect the next generations of your life. Most of all, with great reverence, tell Him that for His glory you are not willing to live without His gracious deliverance from all bitterness. We must accept personal responsibility for our own disobedience and in repentant faith trust the cleansing of the blood of Christ. As you praise Him for the good that He can work out of your pain, the healing process can begin.

CHAPTER TWENTY-FIVE

SEEING GOD'S GOODNESS IN YOUR PAIN

As a nineteen-year-old boy, I begun to follow the Lord for the first time in a whole-hearted way. And after giving my testimony in a church, a sweet lady came up to me and exclaimed, "Great suffering is ahead for you." That statement created fear in my heart and for months afterwards a great gloom would come over me whenever I heard someone speak of trials and suffering. One morning the Spirit of God illuminated 2 Corinthians 1:5 to my soul. It says:

> For just as the sufferings of Christ are ours in abundance, so also our comfort is abundant through Christ.

The thought that this verse plastered on my mind was: "Never fear what might happen because God's comfort will always be there and it will be sufficient!" When we have a clear conscience, a godly perspective, and understand that the battle is the Lord's, we can agree with Peter's words:

> And who is there to harm you if you prove zealous for what is good? But even if you should suffer for the sake of righteousness, you are blessed. (1 Pet. 3:13-14)

Benefits of Trials and Sufferings

To Know God

We observe Paul and Silas praising God after they had been cruelly beaten and thrown in prison (Acts 16:25). This is not to say their suffering was pleasant. It simply affirms that God reveals Himself in a special way to the suffering believer who responds in submission and faith.

God and Father of our Lord Jesus Christ

As Paul reflects on his suffering, he blesses God in 2 Corinthians 1:3 and describes Him in three ways. The first title is: "The God and Father of our Lord Jesus Christ." God has supremely revealed Himself in the Person of the Lord Jesus. Trials can lead us to a knowledge of Christ, and it is this knowledge that conforms us to His moral character (Rom. 8:29). A law that God has established is that you become like that upon which you focus. If you are bitter at someone, you gradually take on the characteristics of that person. If you focus on the Lord's sovereignty and goodness in your trials, you will become like Him (2 Cor. 3:18).

You can experience His peace in your affliction as He promised (John 16:33) by focusing on the One Who is the Source of true peace and Who experienced peace which He calls "rest for your souls" (John 14:27; Matt. 11:29). This kind command, "Be anxious for nothing," and the promise of peace in Philippians 4:6-7 was not initially spoken from a pulpit but written from a prison! This "peace of God" comes from knowing that the believer in Christ has "peace with God" because of His death for our sins and from learning to cast our cares upon Him (Rom. 5:1, I Pet. 5:7). God keeps the believer in perfect peace as our minds are fixed on Him in a posture of trust (Isa. 26:3).

The believer who focuses on the Lord in the midst of trials can also experience the joy of the Lord (John 15:11). This is the joy that is born out of affliction (John 16:21-22) and comes from living in harmony with God. For this reason Christ, who is called the "man of sorrows", is also called the most joyous person who ever lived (Heb. 1:9)!

Father of Mercies

In the midst of his suffering, Paul praises the God who desires to reveal Himself to you as the One whose heart feels for you in all your distress, misery, and weakness. This mercy is so valuable that it is called "rich" (Eph. 2:4) and so understanding that it is called "tender" (Luke 1:78). What are some evidences that you are getting to know God as the "Father of mercies" (2 Cor. 1:3)?

- It is when your trials lead you to a perspective that it is His mercy alone that has delivered you from an eternity of torment (1 Tim. 1:13; cf. Luke 16:24, Ps 73). In your trials praise Him for having saved you from hell.

- It is when you learn to become totally candid with Him about the struggles and temptations of your soul (Heb. 4:16). In your trials tell Him what is on your heart. Are you fearful? Angry? Talk to Him about it.

- It is when you cry out to Him in your spiritual conflicts (Matt. 15:22). Call upon Him to give you strength and wisdom today in your present trials.

- It is when you look to Him each moment of each day to keep you encouraged so that you do not give up (2 Cor. 4:1). Look to God today for your encouragement and endurance to keep going (Rom. 15:5).

- It is when you look to him to comfort you in your times of great concern (Phil 2:27). If you or your loved ones are very sick or suffering, ask God to be a God of mercy to them and to you!

- It is when you yield the totality of your life to the Lord (Rom. 12:1). If He is a God of mercy, whom else would you desire to give your life to?

God of all Comfort

Your trials can allow you to get to know the Source of all comfort. Every good and perfect gift comes ultimately from

Him (James 1:17). Look to Him in all your distress, depression, and times of need. Any thought that "nobody cares" or thoughts of hopelessness do not come from the "God of all comfort" (2 Cor. 1:3).

God is the One who aids, assists, and soothes the believer in his afflictions. But how does He do it? He works through the Holy Spirit who is called in the Greek the "Paracletos"— One who is called alongside to help or comfort. That is why Luke writes of the "comfort of the Holy Spirit" resting upon those who fear God (Acts 9:31).

The Holy Spirit uses two primary sources to comfort: One of these is the Word of God (Rom. 15:4). Trials can open up the Scriptures, and for this reason the Psalmist says:

- This is my comfort in my affliction, that Thy word has revived me. (Ps. 119:50)

- It is good for me that I was afflicted, that I may learn of Thy statutes. (Ps. 119:71)

- Even though princes sit and talk against me, Thy servant meditates on Thy statutes. (Ps. 119:23)

The Holy Spirit also works through people. The apostle states this in this way:

> ...I am filled with comfort. I am overflowing
> with joy in all our affliction. For when we came
> into Macedonia our flesh had no rest, but we
> were afflicted on every side: conflicts without,
> fears within. But God, who comforts the
> depressed, comforted us by the coming of
> Titus. (2 Cor. 7:4-6)

God worked through Titus to give him news of the Corinthians' repentant response to his letter. Titus was also comforted by the Church of Corinth (2 Cor. 7:7). Trials can be used of God to help us know God—the God and Father of our Lord Jesus Christ, the Father of Mercies, and the God of all comfort.

To Learn to Lean on God

We do not know exactly what Paul's trial was that he referred to in 2 Corinthians 1:8. Some have suggested such things as one of his shipwrecks, persecution, a deadly sickness, or even anxiety over the church. What we do know is what he states in 1:9 "indeed, we had the sentence of death within ourselves in order that we should not trust in ourselves, but in God who raises the dead."

It is hard to learn the truth of Christ's words, "Apart from me, you can do nothing" (John 15:5). God uses trials to keep us weak so that we can "[prove] our faith" (1 Pet. 1:6-7). Ron Dunn said that Jesus is all you need, but you will never know it until He is all you have. Our temptation is to try to do for ourselves and others what only God can do.

Whatever makes you rely on God, thank Him for it. From His perspective it is the greatest thing you have going for you. Call upon Him in your day of trouble and He will respond to your repentant cry and you will honor Him. (Ps. 50:15).

As we look to God in our trials He develops the quality of perseverance in our lives (Rom. 5:3; Jas. 1:3). God is the One who gives this staying power, which is needed to receive all He has promised (Rom. 15:5; Heb. 10:36). Abraham Lincoln was an example of perseverance. He was defeated in his bid for the state legislature of Illinois in 1832. He greatly failed in his business efforts and it took him seventeen years to pay off his debts. He fell in love and got engaged, but his fiancée died. He had a nervous breakdown. He was defeated in his race for Congress, and his effort to get an appointment for the U.S. Land Office failed. He ran for Senator but was defeated. He was a candidate for Vice President in 1856 but failed. In 1858 he was defeated by Douglas for President. Only after all of these setbacks did he become the President of the United States.

Let your trials draw you to the Lord. All areas of life attest to the need for perseverance. What if the famous football coach, Vince Lombardi, had believed an 'expert' who evaluated him with these words, "He possesses minimal football knowledge; lacks motivation." What if Beethoven had believed his teacher who called him "hopeless in composition" because he handled the violin awkwardly and preferred playing his own composition rather than improving his technique? Walt Disney was fired by a newspaper for lacking ideas and went bankrupt several times before he built Disneyland. The teacher of the famous opera singer Enrico Caruso said that he had no voice at all and could not sing. Louisa May Alcott, the author of *Little Women*, was advised by her family to find work as a servant. Trials are designed by God to wean us away from a self-trust and to encourage us to look to Him.

To Enhance Your Ministry

When I was interviewing for a pastoral internship with Ben Haden, who at that time was pastor of the famous First Presbyterian Church of Chattanooga, Tennessee, he asked me, "Has God ever broken your heart?" He continued, "That is the preparation for ministry because you will be ministering to people with broken hearts." God comforts us in our trials so that we can overflow with this comfort for others in their trials (2 Cor. 1:3-5).

I remember talking to a dear man who had been rejected by his wife and her parents. He told me that one night he had a pistol to his head, but somehow he did not go through with it. As he reflected on this difficult time he said, "Before this year I didn't know where John 3:16 was, but in His mercy He has opened up the Bible to me." In his agony of deep rejection he became a minister of comfort to others.

As a wife lives with and endures the misunderstanding of an unbelieving husband, she can communicate Jesus to him through her gentle and quiet spirit (1 Pet. 3:1-2). Trials can have a purifying effect on our lives to keep us from pride and enable us to experience more of His grace as we learn to live not to please ourselves and the crowd but rather to do His will (1 Cor. 12:7-19; 1 Pet. 4:1-2). As the Psalmist writes: "Before I was afflicted I went astray, but now I keep Thy Word" (Ps. 119:67).

Much of ministry occurs in times of trials. In prayer, will you ask God to open your heart to receive the revelation of Himself as your Father of mercies and God of all comfort? Trust Him for His gift of endurance (Romans 15:5) in your present trial, and open your life to whatever ministry He has for you. Through the grace of God, you can discover God's goodness in your pain and lead many others to discover the same.

CHAPTER TWENTY-SIX

EXPERIENCING DELIVERANCE FROM BITTERNESS THROUGH PRAYER

Jesus said, "Whenever you stand praying, forgive, if you have anything against anyone…" (Mark 11:25). D.L. Moody said that the one sin that is doing more to hold back the power of God in revival than any other sin is an unforgiving spirit. One night as I knelt down beside my bed in my dorm room to pray, the Spirit of God convicted my conscience with the thought of my anger toward an individual. The scary thing is that if you would have asked me prior to this moment, "Are you angry at this person?" I would have said, "No." Furthermore, I would not have been knowingly trying to deceive you or myself. We need to invite the Spirit of God to reveal the bitterness in our hearts as we seek the Lord with an open Bible. The truth of the matter was that I was bitter toward that person.

God's one clear warning to a husband is not to be bitter toward his wife (Col. 3:19). His one clear warning to a father is not to provoke his child to anger (Col. 3:21). There is no person who does not struggle with anger in some way. Everyone may not express it in the same way, but the temptation to succumb to unrighteous anger and attempt to selfishly vindicate oneself does not bypass anyone.

People tend to either express anger in very active ways, in passive ways or both. Some active expressions include criticism, sarcasm, name-calling, gossip, condemning, accusing, humiliation, ostracizing, pornography, verbal outbursts, threats, intimidation, graffiti, homosexuality, prostitution, honest rage, violence, assault, rape, suicide, murder and terrorism. Some of the passive ways include silence, withdrawal, avoidance, procrastination, half-heartedness, stubbornness, exasperation, drugs and alcohol, jealousy, depression, laziness, and resentment. Let the Lord reveal any unrighteous way you are processing the pain of your soul.

Anger is a wrong response to hurt. While anger that is aimed solely at honoring the glory of God may be righteous, all attempts of personal revenge are not righteous. Some people are created with a greater degree of sensitivity than others and have an even greater capacity to feel hurt. All of us were created with the need for genuine love, but all of us do not have the same capacities.

I remember the testimony of a godly missionary who was going through some challenging times in his life, marriage and ministry. Since the counseling he was receiving was not enabling him to make any progress, he was driven to the Scriptures. Out of his struggle and his study he came up with insights that he developed into a seminar entitled, "Scriptural Solutions for Sensitive People". He noted that God creates people with different capacities. God created some of us as teacups, some of us as glasses, some of us as buckets, and some of us as barrels. In his analogy the larger capacity was associated with the greater sensitivity. He realized that he was a barrel and very sensitive. Any part of God's design for any one of us is a gift of God, but any gift of God can be distorted by Satan. In other words, his extra sensitivity was a gift of God, but the devil was using it to preoccupy him with past hurts.

An illustration that contrasts the two extremes may throw some light on this concept. A teacup is a "matter of fact" person. They are very stable. You may be this kind of person or have a close relationship with one like this. They tend to need to work at developing a little more sensitivity and the ability to express kindness and compassion. They get up; they go to work; and with rock like stability they complete their tasks and then they do the same the next day. Imagine giving this person a totally unexpected phone call one day. You tell him, "I just wanted to call and let you know I was thinking of you and that I love you." Their response might be, "Do you want something?" "No." is your reply, "I only wanted you to know that I was thinking about you." They might hang up and think, "I wonder why in the world they called," and then continue their work. Now the barrel, the most sensitive person, may need several of these kinds of calls each day in order for them not to think that you have rejected them.

It may be that these opposites get together in a relationship. One party admires the great stability in the other person, while the other admires the great sensitivity and compassion in them. The "teacup" may not in any way understand how he or she is hurting the "barrel". The barrel may not realize the unrealistic expectations they are placing on the teacup. While each one of us does need to work at understanding and developing ourselves and those that we relate to, the only lasting solution is learning to look to **Jesus** to continually fill our container no matter what its size. This missionary spoke of the need to come to God's Word every day and to learn about God's love for him and to let his mind dwell on His love almost every minute. "If anyone thirsts, let him come to Me and drink," our Lord said (John 7:37).

How are you processing your pain? Is there a tape recorder playing in the recesses of your mind and you just cannot find the off button? Christ desires to put His healing hand on the hurts of your soul. This healing is not dependent on another person's perfect understanding of you. It is dependent upon your coming to the Lord in complete honesty and opening yourself up to Him and His truth. God will also use other people in your life. Open yourself up to others with the security that you are ultimately placing yourself in the hands of your perfect God. Let Him fill your life with His love and understanding.

In her book, *Glenda's Story: Led by Grace,* Glenda Revell explains:

> Sexual defilement of a child is a monstrous sin, and the rape of a child's spirit is on equal footing. The damage from either would appear irreversible. But

as Dr. David Jeremiah has said, "Our God has the power to reverse the irreversible." It is true, for I have tasted of His cure from both, and it fills me with a longing for Him that the happiest of childhoods could not have given.[20]

At this moment, countless numbers of people are being hurt and abused in a world that is in rebellion against God. Children are being neglected and people are engaged in countless other acts of cruelty. You and I cannot snap our fingers and stop all of this. In God's perfect timing He will intervene in judgment and set up His Kingdom, but today we have the privilege of coming to a loving Father with our hurt and introducing others to the One who is so great and good that He can heal our hurt and even work it together for our eternal good (Rom. 8:28)! May God work on your behalf in a very special way!

---

[20] Glenda Revell, *Glenda's Story: Led by Grace* (Lincoln, Neb.: Gateway to Joy, 1997) p. 41.

CHAPTER TWENTY-SEVEN

LIVING UNDER AN UNCLOUDED HEAVEN

Susan felt a deep compassion for her friend Bonnie who had no place to live because of some difficult circumstances in her life. Acting upon this compassion, Susan and her husband Bob asked Bonnie to come and live with them until she could get her feet back on the ground. After Susan took a brief trip to take care of a family emergency, she returned home to discover that Bonnie had stolen her husband's heart and they had moved out with a plan to get married.

Anyone's "human" reaction to this experience would not be forgiveness. Even for **much** lesser offences, our desire is to create justice ourselves, take vengeance into our own hands, and even find a sadistic pleasure in the pain of the one who has caused us pain. For this reason we need to come with freedom to the throne of grace and talk to the Lord about our pain! Susan has indeed experienced God's miraculous healing touch and is not a bitter woman. Her reaction is beyond a merely "human" response, and she is a walking miracle.

How does God motivate us to forgive? How can one be moved to do what a part of that person has no interest in doing? God's word instructs us about the negative consequences of failing to forgive.

One Who Is Unwilling to Forgive Opens Up His Life to the Torment of Satan

> Be angry, and yet do not sin; do not let the sun go down on your anger, and do not give the devil an opportunity. (Eph. 4:26-27)

When one goes to bed angry, it gives an opportunity to the devil to do a destructive work in one's life. The devil came to steal, kill, and destroy; but Christ came to give us an abundant life (John 10:10). Would you invite a robber who was knocking at your door to come in and plunder your house and loved ones?

Our Lord taught that when we who are forgiven fail to offer forgiveness to others, we are handed over to the torturers (Matt. 18:21-35; see 18:34). This parable is teaching the same principle as Ephesians 4:26-27. The word translated "torturers" is used in the verb form in Revelation 9:5 to refer to demonic torments. One who is bitter opens himself up to being tormented by fear, lusts, and thoughts of self-rejection.

One Who Is Unwilling to Forgive Will Be Plagued with Guilt and Unable to Pray

Our Lord taught that when you pray you should have a heart of forgiveness. When there is bitterness in our hearts, we are not in a position to receive God's cleansing which is conditional upon our walking in the light and confessing our sin (1 John 1:7, 9). There is no feeling as helpless as knowing that our communion with God is blocked because of our unwillingness to cry out to Him about our bitterness.

One Who Is Unwilling to Forgive Will Be under the Negative Influence of the One Against Whom This Bitterness Is Directed

When you or your loved ones have been wronged it is a challenge not to fixate upon the one who hurt you. There are many laws that are part of God's creative design of the universe, and just as true as the law of gravity, is the principle of becoming like the one upon whom we focus. As we behold God's glorious Person we are transformed into His moral likeness (2 Cor. 3:18). Bitterness is like a chain that links one to the negative influence of another.

Bitterness opens one up to many negative influences. It can affect one not only spiritually but also emotionally and physically. Listen to the book of Proverbs which links the condition of our inner person to our physical health:

> A joyful heart is good medicine,
> But a broken spirit dries up the bones. (Prov. 17:22)

> The spirit of a man can endure his sickness,
> But as for a broken spirit who can bear it? (Prov. 18:14)

Bitterness can drain one's physical energy and even increase sickness.

How would someone like Susan ever be able to conquer bitterness and let her thoughts dwell upon that which is true and lovely and worthy of praise (Phil. 4:8). The following chapter will provide the building blocks for this transformation. May this be used in your life and your ministry.

CHAPTER TWENTY-EIGHT

CRYING OUT TO GOD FOR SUPERNATURAL STRENGTH

It was the year 1947, and the place was Munich, Germany. Corrie ten Boom observed a heavyset man wearing a grey overcoat over a blue uniform and a visored cap. The sight of this guard brought back a series of painful memories of her time in the concentration camp where she had experienced great humiliation. She and her sister Betsie had been arrested for concealing Jews in their home in Holland during the Nazi occupation of her country. This man, who had been a guard at the Ravensbruck Concentration Camp, had come to hear her speak on forgiveness.

"A fine message, Fraulein! How good it is to know that, as you say, all our sins are at the bottom of the sea!" These were the words of the guard as he thrust out his hand to Corrie. Since this was the first time since her release, to come face to face with the ones who had so abused her and were responsible for the death of her sister, she simply could not respond.

The guard continued, "You mentioned Ravensbruck in your talk. I was a guard there. But since that time I have become a Christian. I know that God has forgiven me for the cruel things I did there, but I would like to hear it from your lips as well. Fraulein, will you forgive me?"

Corrie stood there observing the guard's outstretched hand as he asked for her forgiveness. As she wrestled in her spirit, she silently prayed to God, "Jesus help me! I can lift out my hand, I can do that much. You supply the feeling." She cried out, "I forgive you brother, with all my heart!" Corrie noted that she had never known God's love so intensely as at that moment.

Why does God desire you to be a channel of His forgiveness to those who have hurt you or hurt one you deeply love? When He asks you to forgive, it does not mean that He is indifferent to your hurt. It does mean that He desires to relieve you of the burden of carrying upon your shoulders the responsibility to create justice. He desires you to lay this burden upon Him. It may be appropriate for you to confront the one who wronged you but not in a spirit of vengeance. God's command for us to forgive comes from His loving devotion to our eternal welfare.

How do you view the one who has hurt you? The natural way is to see them as someone who hurt you! The supernatural way is to see them as a hurting person to whom God may be leading you to minister. Only God can enable and make us willing to minister to someone as He enabled Corrie ten Boom.

A very humbling truth is the fact that no one really has the power to make you angry. We cannot let the flaws of another person justify our unrighteous anger. The individual whom we may be blaming is being used by God to reveal unresolved issues in our own soul. As humbling as it may be, let the Lord show you any unresolved guilt and bitterness in your soul for He will always give grace to the humble.

As I was struggling to have a right attitude towards someone, I began to ponder my lecture notes on anger. I realized that I was exhausted in my spirit. I told the Lord I was tired of trying to be godly and weary of trying to work up the right attitude. In this moment as I was walking on LaSalle Street in Chicago, an insight came into my mind. I temporarily forgot about trying to be forgiving and began to praise God that He who knew everything about me had so graciously forgiven me in Christ. As I praised God, fresh strength came into my soul. As you seek to trust God to build the attitude of forgiveness in your heart, do not lose sight of what God has done for you. He is not asking us to do for others what He has not first so graciously done for us. Martyn Lloyd-Jones stated, "I say to the glory of God and in utter humility that whenever I see myself before God and realize even something that my blessed Lord has done for me, I am ready to forgive anybody anything." He desires to be intimate with us even though we have offended Him in countless ways with our words, attitudes and actions. Glenda, a victim of abuse as a child, shares how God illuminated her mind of God's forgiveness:

> He showed me Calvary once more...I saw the horror
> of my sin, nailing the Son of God to that miserable
> cross, torturing Him, mocking Him, spitting on Him.
> Yet He had forgiven me freely.   No one had
> committed such atrocities against me. How could I
> do anything less than forgive?
>
> Forgiveness came.   And with it came healing,
> complete peace and freedom--absolute freedom--to
> serve my God and to enjoy His love and peace now
> and forevermore.[21]

Praise can put spiritual strength into your soul! God can
also give you hope and victory in areas in which you have
previously failed. How does one avoid experiencing the
same spiritual failure repeatedly? I have known what it is
like to respond wrongly to a situation, feel remorseful after
being convicted, genuinely confess to God my sin, and then
once again at a later date respond in the same incorrect
manner. It is almost as if we have wrongly programmed
responses built into our lives. The good news is that Jesus
shed His blood on the cross to not only forgive us but also
to give us authority to live a new life. God implanted a fresh
hope in my spirit when I began to trust Him on the basis of
Christ's victorious death and resurrection to build new
patterns of thinking and responses into these areas of
repeated failure.

---

[21] Glenda Revell, *Glenda's Story: Led by Grace* (Lincoln, Neb.: Gateway to
Joy, 1997). 98

What does it mean to truly forgive a person? That was the question I was asking myself as I struggled one night. Not wanting to go to bed angry, I committed that person to the Lord and told Him that I was making a willing choice to release this person to Him and give up my right "to even the score". As I released this person to the Lord, I prayed, "Lord, I even reluctantly ask You to bless this person, but if You are looking for somebody to use to do this in their life, don't count on me." As I uttered this prayer I realized that I was still angry and not truly forgiving. True forgiveness involves not only releasing that person to the Lord but also giving ourselves to the Lord as a willing instrument of good in his life. Now what this involves is a blank slate that we must let the Lord fill out. It may mean only praying for them. It could mean confronting them. In this case I sensed God wanted me to give them an encouraging phone call that night. As I was dialing the numbers, my spirit was set free. In this case the painful misunderstanding was resolved, but in every case we can commit the outcome to God and as far as it depends on us be at peace with all men (Rom. 12:18). Sometimes one can build the bridge of reconciliation and the other party may choose not to cross over.

Antoine Rutayisire, an African Christian leader, describes what happened to him as a child:

> When I was five years old my father was butchered in broad daylight, before our very eyes, and left for dead in front of our house. He later on recovered, but was taken once more, and we never saw him again. We don't know how, where and when, or by whom he was killed. He was taken by the chief of

our commune (county) with many other Batutsi and some suspected Bahutu accused of supporting the "enemy" and we were told they had been shot.

We never saw his body, we were never able to bury it. This kept us in a state of suspense for many years, hoping that maybe he had escaped and would come back some day. The death of a dear one is very difficult to accept when you have not witnessed it, or at least have evidence like a grave to prove it. I grew up thinking maybe my father was somewhere and would come back. When they talked of his death my young heart and mind could not accept it. Today I can understand many people who feel the same way, because they do not have any evidence of the death of their dear ones.

When I finally came to accept my father's death I turned my anger on the people I had seen beating my father and looting our possessions. Every time I had a problem I always remembered the massacre scene, and blamed my problem on the people. "If they had not killed my father, I wouldn't be faced with such a problem", was my simplified way of thinking.

I grew even to hate their children and I remember I used to persecute one of them who was with me in secondary school. He was far younger and did not even understand why I hated him and I never took pains to explain.

Then during the massacres of 1972-73 we had to undergo a series of humiliating escapes, spending

> sleepless nights in hiding, uncertain of the future. I
> survived the experience, but this added to my list of
> enemies to hate. The tree of ethnic hatred in my
> heart was growing branches.[22]

Although many of Antoine's relatives were killed, his life
was spared, and after going to college, he became a lecturer
at the National University of Rwanda at Butare. After a year
at the job, he was abruptly fired because the government
decided there were too many lecturers from his ethnic
background. Out of boredom, he began to read the Bible
through several times. The theme of forgiveness gripped
him, but the issue of giving up his bitterness and anger
against the people who had murdered his family seemed
impossible. However, he said, "The fellowship with God
was becoming so precious to me that I didn't want to
jeopardize it by refusing to hand over my anger to God."[23]
He states:

> I took a day alone and sat to forgive and pray for the
> Lord's blessing on all the people I hated. I made a
> list of all their names with all the wrongs each had
> done to me or to my family. Then I started declaring
> forgiveness to each, one by one and calling the
> Lord's blessing on them, their children, their
> businesses and their relatives.

---

[22] Antoine Rutayisire. *Faith Under Fire.* (Essex, Africa Enterprises 1995).
105,106
[23] Ibid. 107

It was a very painful exercise and I had to do it again and again. But the result was tremendous. I was released and healed from the inside and I no longer felt the gripping pang of bitterness whenever one of the old "enemies" was mentioned in my presence.[24]

If you desire the grace of prayer in your ministry, you must take seriously Christ's words, "Whenever you stand praying, forgive, if you have anything against anyone..." (Mark 11:25). May God do a miracle in you and through you every day.

---

[24] Ibid.

CHAPTER TWENTY-NINE

SHARING OUR NEEDS AND DESIRES WITH GOD IN PRAYER

In one of the Los Angeles riots that followed the Rodney King verdict, Reginald Denny was dragged from his truck and maliciously beaten by an angry gang. After a very painful recovery he met with his attackers to shake hands and offer his forgiveness. Such action is difficult to grasp. In fact one reporter's explanation was that Mr. Denny was suffering from brain damage.

Dmitri was a pastor who was beaten in a Romanian prison with a hammer before the dictator Ceausescu was ousted. His body was paralyzed so that he could move only his neck. In the prison there was no nurse to take care of him, no wife or mother to change his linens, and no loving hands during the day to even offer him a cup of water. He would lie in his human waste as he awaited his fellow prisoners to return from slave labor to help him drink a cup of water.

After lying in his prison for two years experiencing what could be termed "hell on earth," he was released in December 1989 when the dictator was ousted. While he was still unable to move either his hands or feet, he now had other loving hands to help him.

One day the communist who had crippled him appeared at his door. He said, "Sir, don't believe that I have come to ask forgiveness from you. For what I have done, there is no forgiveness, not on earth or in heaven. You are not the only one I have tortured like this. You cannot forgive me; nobody can forgive me. Not even God! My crime is much too great. I have come only to tell you that I am sorry about what I have done. From you I go to hang myself. That is all."

As he turned to leave, Pastor Dmitri said, "Sir, in all these years I have not been as sorry as I am now, that I cannot move my arms. I would love to stretch them out to you and embrace you. For years I have prayed for you every day. I love you with all of my heart. You are forgiven."[25]

These individuals had come to experience the grace of God and miracle of forgiveness. Forgiveness was not denying that they were hurt or simply attempting to bury their painful experience so as to push it out of their mind. It was an act of their will to obey God's command to forgive, motivated and enabled by God's grace in prayer.

As one walks in humble transparency before the Lord, one can experience His aid. Walking down the street one day with me, Sean began to share the insight that he had been learning. He noted that previously when he was struggling

---

[25] Richard Wurmbrand, "Give Me a Gem of Christian", *Voice of the Martyrs,* December 1998, 14.

with temptation he envisioned God up in heaven observing how he would respond in the struggle. Now he said, "It is not God up in heaven observing me but it is God right here with me aiding me and fighting **our** common enemy." David had the courage to fight Goliath because he did not perceive it as Goliath versus David, rather Goliath versus God. Put that which most readily tempts you to become bitter into God's hand and let Him win His victory. It is our responsibility to walk in the light before God with no "secret" sins.

We will better understand ourselves when we come to grips with the truth that God has created each one of us with certain needs, such as: the need to be loved, the need to feel secure, the need to be appreciated and the need to be understood. There is nothing sinful about these legitimate needs nor can we come to the place where they are no longer present in our heart. What we do with these needs is another matter. We can turn them into demands on other people. In a relationship, we can transfer our need to be loved and appreciated into a demand to which the other person must respond in a certain way to make us feel loved and appreciated. When this expectation or demand is not met, anger is the natural response. This anger stems from taking legitimate, God-given needs and turning them into demands and expectations.

The currents of our anger flow in one of three directions. When we take our needs and turn them into demands which God must meet a certain way according to a certain timetable, we set ourselves up to be bitter toward God. In our mind, God is not really good because He did not come through according to our expectation. When we turn these needs into expectations that we place upon others, we will ultimately be disappointed and angry at other people. As a result, this expectation can easily destroy relationships. Thirdly, we can even put wrong demands upon ourselves which result in frustration over not being able to live up to those demands. Our anger can be directed towards God, others, or ourselves.

How does one deal with these God-given needs in a godly way? It involves first yielding, presenting, or offering something to God. What do we yield? We must yield our desires to God. It requires a knowledge of God to trust Him with our desires. Hopefully you have a long enough track record to realize that some of your desires can be very shortsighted and even deceitful. What you may have greatly struggled with as a junior high student may not be as great a concern to you thirty years later.

Some of our desires can be surface desires. To call them surface desires is not at all to belittle them but simply to affirm that you have stronger desires beneath them. When the apostle Paul repeatedly petitioned God to remove his thorn in the flesh, it reflected a surface desire. However, God did not answer this prayer in the way he requested in order to give him a greater desire—to experience more of God's grace and power (2 Cor. 12:7-10)!

Tony Dungy is the head coach of the Indianapolis Colts. In speaking to the hundreds who had gathered in the fourth floor ballroom at the Marriott Renaissance in Detroit, Michigan, on the morning before Super Bowl XL, he shared about the lessons he had learned from his sons

He spoke of his middle son, Eric, who he said shares his competitiveness and who is focused on sports "to where it's almost a problem." He spoke of his youngest son, Jordan, who has a rare congenital condition which causes him not to feel pain. "He feels things, but he doesn't get the sensation of pain," Dungy said.

The lessons learned from Jordan, Tony Dungy said, are many. "That sounds like it's good at the beginning, but I promise you it's not," Dungy said. "We've learned some hurts are really necessary for kids. Pain is necessary for kids to find out the difference between what's good and what's harmful."

Jordan, Dungy said, loves cookies. "Cookies are good," Dungy said, "but in Jordan's mind, if they're good out on the plate, they're even better in the oven. He will go right in the oven when my wife's not looking, reach in, take the rack out, take the pan out, burn his hands and eat the cookies and burn his tongue and never feel it. He doesn't know that's bad for him." Jordan, Dungy said, "has no fear of anything, so we constantly have to watch him." The lesson learned, Dungy said, is simple.

"You get the question all the time, "Why does the Lord allow pain in your life? Why do bad things happen to good people? If God is a God of love, why does he allow these hurtful things to happen?" Dungy said. "We've learned that a lot of times because of that pain, that little temporary pain, you learn what's harmful. You learn to fear the right things."[26]

We are to also yield our expectations and demands we place on others to God. One might ask, "Is it always wrong to have expectations of others?" Certainly not, but what may make it wrong is the motivation behind them. It is certainly not wrong for a parent to expect his child to obey him. However, if his motivation for the child's obedience is only to make the parent look good and not the child's well-being, then the unmet expectation will result in anger.

We may even need to yield to God the illegitimate demands we are placing on ourselves. Jesus tells us that truth will set us free because it can free us from the bondage of wrong ideas. I remember a godly man coming to me one day and describing his frustration as he sought to please a key person in his life. "Every time I am around this man it appears that he is never pleased with anything I say or do," he exclaimed. As we talked, we identified the lie that controlled him—"It is my responsibility to make this man happy." This is a lie, for it places a demand upon one that he cannot handle. In fact it allows the other person's response to determine whether or not we can have a good day. This lie needed to be replaced with the truth—"It is my responsibility to be a channel of God's love to this man and I will trust God with his response but will not take responsibility for it." This man was set free.

---

[26] The source of this story was an anonymous article that was emailed to me. (Article originally appeared Saturday, February 4, 2006, "Spreading His Message," www.Colts.com)

When one genuinely yields his desires and demands to the Lord in prayer, he will always gain. First of all he gains a freedom from idolatry and a freedom to look to God. He created man as a dependent creature with needs that He alone can ultimately fulfill. An idol is that to which one looks to meet the thirsts of one's heart. An idol can be a person, a position, a possession, or even a practice. We can idolize a relationship, a job, a car, a home, food, sex, or entertainment. When we look to anything but God, we will be ultimately disappointed. "The sorrows of those who have bartered for another god will be multiplied" (Psalm 16:4). Jesus instructs us to come to Him with our thirsty hearts and He can abundantly satisfy us (John 7:37-39).

When one yields his desires and demands to the Lord, he also gains a freedom to live before Him. He will not experience a "light load" living before the opinions of people. Only Jesus can promise this as we live under His yoke (Matt. 11:28-30). Christ wants to experientially teach each one of us that He is a **wonderful** Master and that we can be a cruel master for our lives. The Bible says that he who trusts in his own heart is a fool (Prov. 28:26a). When something means a lot to you, there is tendency to try to take the matter into your own hands and attempt to solve your own problems. When we are hurt by someone there is the temptation to think that it is up to us to create the justice. This can become an unbearable load. To be sure God not only feels every hurt of His children but will also ultimately right every wrong. There will one day be a "revelation of the righteous judgment of God" (Rom. 2:5) because "lying lips are only for a moment but the truth will be established forever" (Prov. 12:19).

Yielding our desires and demands to God also leads to the freedom to be grateful. What would you and I be experiencing at this moment if we were getting what we deserved? We would be in a place of eternal torment experiencing unbearable pain and utter loneliness. Anything that ever comes our way other than the "torment" that we have earned is due to God's grace. An understanding of God's holiness leads one to realize that all have sinned and earned God's righteous judgment. Jesus' gracious death is God's gift to release us from this penalty. When we yield our demands and expectations to God we are free to be grateful for every good and perfect gift that comes from a gracious God (Jas 1:17). There are two ways of looking at a relationship. One way is to evaluate what the other person is **not** doing for you. The other way is to be grateful for what the other person is doing for you. The freedom to be grateful is the fruit of yielding our demands and desires to God. When we expect or demand people to fully meet our God-given needs we will always be disappointed. However, when we can release these demands to the Lord in prayer then we can celebrate the truth that they are a reflection and an instrument of God. May this be your continual experience.

SECTION FIVE

NEED FOR FREEDOM FROM GUILT—EXPERIENCING THE GRACE OF CONVICTION AND CONTINUAL CLEANSING

Every person whom God has ever created has been given a conscience. In our consciences God implants His eternal moral law. Since no one has ever fully lived up to it, guilt is a universal problem. Only in Christ can one find a solution to his guilt.

Christ's death not only makes possible the forgiveness that brings us into reconciliation with a Holy God but also the continual cleansing that enables the believer to walk with God on a moment-by- moment basis. A soul physician needs to learn to skillfully discern between the adversary's accusation and the kind conviction of the Holy Spirit. He also needs to learn the freedom of walking in the light and maintaining the intense joy of a clear conscience before God. I pray that these next chapters aid you in your personal journey and in your ministry to others.

CHAPTER THIRTY

REALIZING THE KINDNESS OF GOD'S CONVICTION

One cannot experience the grace of God if he is being motivated by guilt. One must learn to deal with guilt God's way, and the first step is to correctly see God's conviction. Samuel was a man with a lovely wife, but he treated her with sarcasm, unusual demands, and even by withdrawing from her love and attention. When he realized he was destroying his marriage, he went to see a counselor. He faced his problem like a real man—he blamed his wife! When he finally got honest he began to see the root of the problem.

During his years in the service he had spent two weeks in Japan to relax during a period of military leave. As he walked the streets of Tokyo, his loneliness and terrible homesickness led him to make a wrong choice. He visited a prostitute several times during this time in Japan.

Samuel was now a pastor but had never been able to forgive himself. When he returned home from his military duty he was welcomed by his faithful fiancée who had waited for him. He never shared his past moral conflicts with anyone and simply could not forgive himself for what he had done. He unconsciously brought the thought into this marriage that he had no right to enjoy his wife. Being tormented by his guilt, he dealt horribly with his wife and hurt his people with excessively harsh and judgmental sermons. [27]

Guilt is a phenomenon with which every person must deal because every person that God has ever created was given a conscience. On this conscience God writes His eternal moral law. The awareness that one has violated this moral law sets off an alarm and the awareness of moral guilt.

How do people respond to this alarm? A person may choose to *suppress* it just as a person can push the snooze button on his alarm clock. The suppression can take the form of trying to *rationalize* it away by *criticizing* or *blaming* others in order to minimize our wrong. One of the results of open rebellion is the desire to throw off all moral restraints. A common antidote is to attempt to do something to *compensate* for our guilt and that becomes guilt-motivated. *Superficial confession* is an attempt to remove the guilt but without any desire or intention to change one's life.

What is a healthy way to respond to one's guilt? If you are an unbeliever there is only one healthy way to respond to the truth of your guilt in breaking God's law: admit your

[27] Seamonds. *Healing for Damaged Emotions.* Victor Books, Wheaton, Ill. 1981, p. 31-32.

guilt and trust Jesus Christ who died as your substitute and paid the penalty for your sin. "For Christ also died for sins once for all, the Just for the unjust" (1 Pet. 3:18).

When a believer sins against God, what is the correct response to his guilt? The first thing that God desires to teach His children is that His conviction of our sins is not to be equated with condemnation. When one trusts Jesus Christ, he is freed from God's condemning wrath (cf. Rom. 8:1).

As God was bringing to my attention a number of issues in my life that needed to change, the response in my mind was, "Lord, when will you leave me alone?" At that moment another thought entered my mind. It was, "I love you so much that I will never leave you alone!" I have never looked at God's conviction in the same way since that day. I am so glad that God has not left me alone. The humbling truth is that even a believer still has the capacity to destroy his life and the relationships in his life.

I have learned to attach the correct meaning to God's conviction. When God convicts us He is saying to us, "I desire you to experience my love." To be sure, God set His love upon us when we were ungodly, helpless, sinners and His enemies (Rom. 5:6-10). While it is true that He has an unconditional love for me, it is also true that an obedient child *experiences* more of God's love. Think of a loving parent dealing with two of his children; one is very obedient and cooperative and the other is very rebellious. The parent *loves* both of his children, but the obedient child *experiences* more of the parent's love. In the same way, God manifests His presence and love to the obedient believer:

> "He who has My commandments and keeps them is
> the one who loves Me; and he who loves Me will be
> loved by My Father, and I will love him and will disclose
> Myself to him." Jesus answered and said to him, "If
> anyone loves Me, he will keep My word; and My
> Father will love him, and We will come to him and
> make Our abode with him. (John 14:21; 23)

As Christ dwells in our hearts, we are able to comprehend
and experience all the dimensions of God's love:

> So that Christ may dwell in your hearts through faith;
> and that you, being rooted and grounded in love, may
> be able to comprehend with all the saints what is the
> breadth and length and height and depth, and to know
> the love of Christ which surpasses knowledge, that you
> may be filled up to all the fullness of God. (Eph. 3:17-
> 19)

If there is someone in your life who is willing to tell you the
truth even when they know you do not desire to hear it, you
have one who truly loves you. God's conviction is a mark of
His love for you. He desires your life to be fruitful. He is not
indifferent to your life.

> My Father is glorified by this, that you bear much fruit,
> and so prove to be My disciples. (John 15:8)

God is eternally satisfied and sufficient. He is not lacking in anything. He is perfect in every way. In His perfect love He desires your fellowship. It means so much to Him, that you be able to enjoy Him for who He is. When your sin hinders this, He lovingly and graciously convicts you.

Why not thank God right now that He has not left you alone? This is God's loving discipline. God desires to convict you and when He does He is saying:

1. I desire that you experience my love.
2. I desire that your life be fruitful and productive.
3. I desire your fellowship and am committed to our relationship.

May you open your life to God's loving conviction and become His instrument so that others might to experience it also.

CHAPTER THIRTY-ONE

FINDING FREEDOM IN WALKING IN THE LIGHT

If one desires to experience the grace of unceasing prayer (1 Thess. 5:17), it is essential to understand the concept of "walking in the light". As a college student, I attended Auburn University. It is located in Auburn, Alabama, which is about fifty miles from my hometown of Montgomery, Alabama. Once a month I would go home for the weekend to fulfill my military obligation with the Air Force Reserve. On one such weekend, I also came with the agenda of sharing the Lord with some boys who lived a few houses down the street from our home. Seeing them in their yard, I walked over and began to engage them in conversation. While they endured my conversation, they did not appear to be very interested.

As I walked back home, a young man approached me on the street and inquired if I could help him find a job. I replied, "I think I can help you." At that time my uncle owned a plumbing company, and I knew that there was a possibility that he might hire a laborer. I asked the young man to come to my home and let me share something with him first. As I shared the gospel he appeared to understand it. When I asked him, "Would you like to trust Christ right now to be *your* Savior?" He replied, "I just can't do it; I just can't do it." After inquiring why he felt he could not trust Christ, he answered, "I do not trust myself. After I leave you I am concerned that I will sin." In his mind he evidently believed that any future sin would "undo" his conversion. In a very elementary way, I explained to him how a Christian deals with his sin. While there was nothing sophisticated about my explanation, the truth hit his heart and he expressed a desire to trust Jesus Christ for his salvation. The fact that Jesus died on the cross—is an historical event, but the genuine belief that Jesus died for me—that's salvation.

After the young man trusted Christ, he began to leap in the air and shout the words, "I have eternal life; I have eternal life!" Then he started walking away. I ran toward him and said, "I told you I would try to help you find a job." He replied, "I have eternal life and that is enough right now." His temporal need had momentarily left him. This young man experienced the *joy* that comes from true fellowship with God (1 John 1:3-4).

The One Perfect Person (1 John 1:5)

Fellowship with God is joyous because it is fellowship with *GOD!* The apostle John's summary of Jesus' message was that "God is light, and in Him there is no darkness" (1 John 1:5). He is the only one of whom you can say that the closer you look the better He looks. There is no blemish in His character. He is perfect in every way: in character, action, words, and motivations. He gives His people the gift of being able to enjoy Him in His perfection--this is true joy. When you and God are walking with each other in agreement, you can experience joy. Because Jesus in His humanity *always* walked in perfect agreement with His heavenly Father, He was the most joyous person who ever lived (cf. Heb. 1:9).

Absence of Hypocrisy, Self-deception and Rationalization (1 John 1:6, 8, 10)

God has provided a way to walk with Him, but how? He declares that it requires an absence of *hypocrisy*. If one professes to have fellowship with God and yet walks in the darkness, he is a liar (1 John 1:6). His life does not match his profession. It is a challenge not to be a hypocrite. When we sing "Sweet Hour of Prayer", is it a reality in our lives? When we sing "Take My Life and Let It Be", do we really mean it? Are you walking in conscious sin? If so, you cannot enjoy fellowship with God because He requires an absence of hypocrisy.

God also requires an absence of self-deception and an absence of rationalization. If we say we have no sin, or in other words, we deny our guilt and our need for the cleansing blood of Jesus, we are living in deceit and God's truth is not having a controlling influence on us (1 John 1:8). In the same way if we fail to agree with God's conviction of our sin by denying it, we are calling God a liar and not letting His Word abide in us (1 John 1:10). The only way to experience the joy of God's fellowship is to live in agreement with Him. This requires not only an absence of hypocrisy but also an absence of self-deception and rationalization.

Walking in the Light (1 John 1:7, 9)

The believer's responsibility is to walk in the light. This involves being *open*, *honest*, and *transparent* before God and His truth. It is the opposite of covering our sin. The Bible gives a promise that is true whether you or I believe it or not. The first part of Proverbs 28:13 declares, "He who conceals his transgressions will not prosper." We are not to try to harbor any secret sin. In some cases, in order for us to truly get a matter into the light, we may need to follow God's counsel in James 5:16: "Confess your sins to one another, and pray for one another." The good news is that you can struggle in the light. Tell the Lord about your temptations and purpose to let every temptation draw you into a conversation with God.

What happens when you walk openly, honestly and transparently before God? According to 1 John 1:7, you can experience continual cleansing of the blood of Jesus. An aspect of walking in the light is explained in 1 John 1:9 as confessing one's sin. This is the opposite of rationalizing our sin and calling God a liar. It is agreeing with God and saying in our hearts, "God, you are right; I have sinned." As you agree with Him, you do not have to beg or plead with God to forgive your sin. He has faithfully promised to respond by forgiving or sending it away. He is also righteous in doing so because Christ's death fully satisfied God's righteousness. Do not try in any way to atone for your sins by any form of penance because Christ's payment is complete!

Scripture speaks of not only the judicial forgiveness of our sins but also what we might call family forgiveness. In 1 John 2:12, the apostle John affirmed that the believers' sins have already been forgiven them. This is the forgiveness that cleansed them from all of their sins—past, present, and future—in order to bring them into a permanent relationship with a holy God. The same believers are instructed to confess their sins in order to experience forgiveness. Why? In 1 John 1:7 and 1:9 he is not talking about the forgiveness of God that brings one into a saving relationship with God but the provision of continual cleansing that allows His redeemed children to walk in fellowship with Him.

The truth of walking in the light is not to lead to an unhealthy introspection. In reverence to God, it is *His* responsibility to point out our sins. It is *our* responsibility to be attentive to His word and agree with His Spirit's conviction. As we do, He forgives us our sin and cleanses us from *all* unrighteousness. This promise releases one from a *continual* self-examination that leads to the tormenting thought, "What if I can't remember a sin I have committed?" We are to walk in the light and be in conscious agreement with the Lord and His truth, and the result is cleansing from *all* unrighteousness.

God will always honor a truly repentant heart. Is it possible to repeatedly commit a sin after confessing it? Genuine confession does imply that you have no willful intention of committing the sin again. However, this does not mean that there may not be future occurrence of this sin. If one confesses as an attempt to only remove his guilt but no desire to change his life, this is not genuine confession because he is not in agreement with God.

When our Lord instructed His disciples to pray, He said to pray: "Forgive us our debts, as we also have also forgiven our debtors" (Matt. 6:12). He was saying that true confession involves dealing with the bitterness in our souls. Our focus on another's sin against us can lead us to not take full responsibility for our sin. An unwillingness to deal with our bitterness can lead us to be tormented by guilt! God is "ready to forgive" according to Psalm 86:5. We noted the *one* time in Scripture that God is pictured as being in a hurry. It is when He is portrayed as the Father of the prodigal son running to restore him. God has His arms open wide and longs to restore you. He even says to those who have committed spiritual adultery against Him, "Draw near to God and He will draw near to you." (James 4:8; cf. James 4:4). Will you draw near to the Lord in prayer right now and ask Him to bring to the light anything that is a barrier in your relationship with Him? May you continue to walk in the light of God and inspire many others to do the same.

CHAPTER THIRTY-TWO

DISCERNING THE DIFFERENCE BETWEEN SATAN'S ACCUSATION AND GOD'S CONVICTION

The grace of prayer is a wonderful gift that comes from a kind God who will lovingly convict us and lead us to experience His provision of continual cleansing as we walk in the light (Chapter 31). We also have a wicked Adversary who will seek to accuse us and distort our enjoyment of God. One night after teaching a three-hour class, I received a ride home from a colleague. I had a nagging and tormenting sense of guilt about something I had said. There did not seem to be anything wrong with the words I had said, but that logic did not seem to silence the torment I felt.

How do we discern the difference between the Spirit of God's conviction and the Adversary's accusation? One name for the devil is the "Accuser of the brethren." There may be times when a single contrast is not sufficient. You may need to use more than one. Here are things that have been a help to me:

Characteristics of the Spirit's Conviction	Characteristics of the Adversary's Accusation
1. **Clear and Specific.** If God expects me to confess my sin, it will be clear and specific enough for a spiritual heart to agree with it. (1 John 1:9)	1. **Vague.** Even after seeking God and godly counsel you cannot quite grab hold of the issue.
2. **Helpful.** God is seeking to aid your life. Even His discipline is motivated by love. (Heb. 12:6)	2. **Harassing.** The Adversary seeks no constructive good for your life.
3. **Hopeful.** God is a God of hope. He not only points out our needs but His solution to those needs. (Rom. 15:13)	3. **Despairing.** The Adversary seeks to preoccupy us with our problem and magnify it so as to attack our faith and hope.
4. **Truthful.** The Holy Spirit is the Spirit of truth, and His conviction will be in harmony with His truth.	4. **Deceitful.** The Adversary is a liar and works in the realm of deceit as he seeks to twist and distort

Characteristics of the Spirit's Conviction	Characteristics of the Adversary's Accusation
(John 15:26)	God's truth.
5. **One thing at a time.** This is related to God's conviction being clear enough and specific enough for an attentive spiritual heart to agree with it in confession. (1 John 1:9)	5. **Many things at once.** This is related to the Adversary's desire to harass one and drive him to despair.
6. **Results in a freedom to love people.** God gives grace as we humbly agree with Him and His Spirit manifests the fruit of love. (Gal. 5:22)	6. **Results in bondage of people.** The Adversary attacks true freedom and seeks to enslave us in fear.

If there is an adversary who accuses, then there is such a thing as false guilt. Let's examine this topic very carefully. Examples of false guilt:

1. **Thinking temptation itself is sin.** Jesus was tempted in all ways yet He was sinless (Matt. 4:1; Heb. 4:15). Temptation itself is not sin, and as long as we live in this

unredeemed body and unredeemed world, we will be tempted.

2. **Not being able to live up to another's illegitimate expectations.** It is important to be freed from letting another be the absolute lord of our life. That place is reserved for God alone. It is important that we obey our authorities, but this is to be done in the fear of the Lord. We are to seek to bring pleasure to the Lord and let this be our greatest priority (Gal. 1:10).

3. **Feeling guilty for things out of one's control.** This seems very logical and it *is* as long as one is objective. However, when one is wrestling with this inside of one's self, it can become subjective and not as clear. One can wrongly feel guilty for the divorce of one's parents, the death of a loved one, or one's abuse as a child.

One can even feel guilty for not being able to make another happy. I mentioned the friend who came to me and related his struggle in relating to an older man in his life. He said, "Every time I am around him, I go out of my way to please him, but I always walk away sensing his displeasure. As we talked, I told him that he had to reject this thought—"It is my responsibility to make this man happy." This lie enabled the older man's response to control him. I told him to replace it with the truth—"It is my responsibility to be a vessel of love to this man and his response is beyond my control and my responsibility." Only as far as it depends on us are we asked to be at peace with all men (Rom. 12:18).

Several Christian writers have noted the helpful difference between desires and goals. A goal is something for which we can assume responsibility. For example, a mother can have the goal of being a godly mother. A desire is something you trust God with and is beyond your ultimate control. For example, the desire of the same mother is to have godly children.

Dynamics of False Guilt

The personal illustration with which I began this chapter taught me a valuable lesson. First of all, I talked it out with my colleague. This is often God's provision for us as He intends for us to live in community. John conferred that he saw nothing wrong with what I had said. As I got out of his car and walked into my apartment, I saw the real issue. There was nothing wrong with what I had said, but the attitude beneath the words was clearly wrong. This often illustrates the dynamic of false guilt. There may be true guilt beneath the false guilt. I attached the guilt of my sinful attitude to the words I had spoken.

After my father went home to be with the Lord, I came home from school to live with my mother for the summer. While working as an associate pastor in a church, I had an intense and even oppressive burden to witness to a man who had been at one time a boss of my father. I attempted to ignore this and continued with my pastoral responsibilities, but the burden was so intense I could not. After a few days of this, I stopped everything and began to seek God. I said, "Lord, this oppression does not seem to be the way that you communicate; but if you want me to witness to this man I will stand on my head and do so!" After this prayer, I realized that before this time of seeking God, I had been unwilling and even fearful of the thought of witnessing to this intimidating man. This possibility was not even on my radar screen. It was this unwillingness that was opening me up to the devil's torment. The only way we can resist the devil is by being fully submitted to God (James 4:7). I saw this man about a week later at an event where the word of God was being proclaimed. It was as if God said to me, "I have no problem getting my word to this man. That is not my concern. My concern is with your being truly available to me to do whatever I would ask you to do."

Seek God at every point of concern. As you walk in the light, He will cleanse you from all sin. Employ the help of another, this may be necessary to truly get the matter into the light and discern God's mind on the issue. If it is God's conviction, it needs to be confessed. If it is not, it needs to be rejected and replaced with truth. Do not fail to look for the possibility that there is an issue beneath the matter with which you are dealing. Be decisive as you seek God. It is not His will for you to live with continual uncertainty. I have seen God honor many times the prayer, "Lord, I lay this matter before you today. I desire to put my head on the pillow tonight with a clear conscience. Show me anything between me and a clear conscience and by your grace I will do it." If there is anything on your heart, why not seek God right now. We will explain the matter of a clear conscience in the next chapter.

CHAPTER THIRTY-THREE

LIVING WITH A CLEAR CONSCIENCE BEFORE GOD

One who experiences the grace of God in his life and ministry seeks to live with a clear conscience before God. Over thirty years ago, I was introduced to the challenge of seeking to live with a clear conscience before God and man. A clear conscience was defined as an inner freedom of spirit and assurance that is derived from knowing that you have a transparency toward everyone because no one is able to point a finger at you and legitimately accuse you of wrongs toward them that you have never made right. I had just graduated from college and the gift of a clear conscience was the greatest graduation present I could have ever received.

As wonderful as this gift of a clear conscience is, we often resist receiving it. Perhaps we do not fully realize the value of the gift. I was told on that warm June evening in Atlanta, Georgia, that it would result in a greater freedom in relationships, an enhanced receptivity to God's leading, and the enablement to experience the victory over temptation that Christ had died to give me. To be sure, every gift— including the gift of a clear conscience--is merited solely by Christ. We are simply to respond to God's Spirit who seeks to lead us into the full experience of what Christ has earned for us.

Interestingly enough, it is the negative consequences of rejecting His truth that usually move us to action more than the positive benefits. The apostle Paul urged Timothy to "keep a good conscience" in order to not follow the example of some who rejected it and "suffered shipwreck in regard to their faith." (1 Tim. 1:19-20) When our conscience is not clear we are not able to rejoice in trials and honor Christ (cf. 1 Pet. 3:16). I have known times when I have opened myself up to burdensome sacrificial actions only to discover that they were not truly motivated by God. Such actions are "dead works" because they have not been motivated by the Lord but only by a guilty conscience.

> Unless the LORD builds the house,
> They labor in vain who build it;
> Unless the LORD guards the city,
> The watchman keeps awake in vain.
> It is vain for you to rise up early,
> To retire late,
> To eat the bread of painful labors;
> For He gives to His beloved even in his sleep. (Ps. 127:1-2)

As you examine the definition of this glorious gift, what are the things that God's Spirit brings to your mind? I was reminded of a number of past acts of dishonesty that I needed to decide that night to get right with the Lord. Ask the Lord to examine your heart and bring to mind any past action that hinders your spirit of transparency toward the Lord or others. Consider such things as:

- Past acts of lying
- Cheating
- Stealing
- Damaging another's reputation
- Rebellion to authorities
- Bitterness and malice toward another
- Losing your temper

Look at these actions in light of your relationship with God, your family, your relatives, your neighbors and friends, your employers and teachers and other acquaintances.

The helpful guidance to me that night was to not rationalize anything away, but to deal with the hardest thing first. This is to aid us in not letting the accuser magnify other things that may lead to false guilt, arising because of our refusal to respond to God's gracious conviction.

The best way to ask forgiveness of a person is in person. They are able to see your facial expression and other non-verbal communication. It gives you the opportunity to clarify yourself when this is necessary. It may be best even to prepare the words you will say, "God has convicted me that I was wrong in _____. I am sorry for my sin. Would you please forgive me? " Place no blame on them. Our first responsibility is to clear our conscience and deal with our sin. Any time we humble ourselves before God by asking forgiveness, He always gives grace:

> But He gives a greater grace. Therefore it says, "GOD IS OPPOSED TO THE PROUD, BUT GIVES GRACE TO THE HUMBLE." (Jas. 4:6)

When it is not possible to ask forgiveness in person, a phone call would be better than a letter. This allows for the other to hear your voice and discern your understanding of how your sin hurt them.

After Onesimus became a Christian under Paul's ministry in Rome, he was also encouraged to clear his conscience. He had run away from his master and stolen from him. The little book of Philemon tells us the story of how Paul did not tell Onesimus to forget his past wrong actions or to only confess them to God, but to respond to the joy of God's complete forgiveness by returning to his master, asking his forgiveness and making restitution. The book Philemon is also evidence of the truth that God will go before us and prepare the way just as Paul did for Onesimus!!

A number of years ago I was backing out of my driveway and waving goodbye to my son. No one ever parks in the street behind our driveway, but they did that day—"Crash."

I got out of the car to check the damage and then proceeded to knock on doors to find the owner of the car I had hit. As they observed the dent in their car they responded, "That dent was already there." What relief I felt! What providence to hit a car where it had already been hit!

As I attended a pastor's conference the next day I still had a heavy heart about this accident. I sensed the need to contact the person again. After finally securing their phone number, I asked them to look at their car and make sure I had truly not done any damage. Once again they affirmed that no new damage had been done.

My mind at once flashed back to an incident in my past. As a high school student I had gone to the county fair with my cousin. Driving out of the parking lot that night, I hit a car. Fear struck me and I raced out of the parking lot. This thing had come to my mind before, but I knew no way I could make it right. However on this day an idea came to mind that I had never thought of before. Since I remembered the month, year and place of the accident, I was prompted to make a long-distance phone call to the police station in the city where I had hit the car many years ago.

As I inquired about whether they had records of past accidents, the gentleman on the phone asked me, "Why do you want to know?"   I replied, "I am ashamed of this, but when I was in high school I hit a car and drove away. If you could help me identify, through your records, the person who owned the car, I would like to make it right with them." He told me that it would take about an hour to look through the records and identify any accident that would match the date and place that I gave him. He promised to call me back.

After an hour had passed and I had not heard from the police station; I made a phone call to them. He described to me the only two cars on record that matched the information. I responded that neither of these was the car I hit. He told me that that was all he could do. As I hung up the phone I began to doubt myself and called my cousin to see if perhaps one of these two cars did fit the description of the car I hit. He remembered the year, make, and color of the car and his information did confirm that it was not either of the cars. In this case there was nothing more I could do but put the matter before the Lord and live in light of His grace.

Hundreds of years ago John Chrysostom said, "The danger is not that we should fall but that we should remain on the ground." God is for you! Respond to His Spirit and let Him lead you into the glorious freedom of a clear conscience before God and man. As you humble yourself before Him, God will allow you to experience His grace, and this includes the grace of prayer and the grace of ministering as a soul physician.

SECTION SIX

*NEED FOR DELIVERANCE
FROM FEAR—EXERIENCING
THE GRACE OF COURAGE AND
FAITH*

As long as you live in this world you will be tempted. Temptation is a common experience to all (1 Cor. 10:13), and fear is a common temptation. One year I sought God and asked him to illuminate my soul to help realize what things I said or did not say and did or did not do that were not motivated by Him but by an unhealthy fear. I discovered that fear was a far greater motivation than I ever realized.

As you read these next chapters, would you ask God to help you get in touch with your battle with fear? Only as you let God aid you in identifying and processing the unhealthy fears of your life will you truly understand the depth of His love for you. Your willingness to open up to the Lord in this way will put you on the pathway to being God's instrument in the lives of others as well. They will thank you for all eternity for leading them into a richer experience of God's amazing love.

CHAPTER THIRTY-FOUR

LETTING YOUR FEARS ENCOURAGE YOU TO SEEK GOD

The grace of prayer is not something that can only be experienced in a quiet room. Just as it can be experienced in your struggle with anger (Section Four) and your struggle with guilt (Section Five), it is also essential to help you process your fears (Section Six). To be tempted is a common experience for every believer. To be tempted to fear is a common and universal temptation. When we talk about fear we need to note that we are not talking about the *purifying fear* of the Lord. The fear of God is not just a fear to keep us from doing the wrong thing but also the corresponding courage to do the right thing. Nor are we talking about *healthy cautions,* such as being afraid of grizzly bears and rattlesnakes. We are talking about *paralyzing fears* that cause us to be afraid to do the right thing.

Many cite the fear of failure as the greatest fear in the life of a man and the fear of rejection as the greatest fear in the life of a woman. To be sure both fears cross gender lines and certainly hinder the experience of intimacy. A man often struggles to lovingly lead his family because his fear is, "If I lead and fail, will I be rejected?" A wife may struggle to show respectful submission to her husband because her fear is, "Can I give of myself in this way without being rejected?" Each of us should ask ourselves, "What are things that I do or do not do and say or do not say that are motivated by a fear of rejection?" You will probably discover, as I have, that fear is a greater motivation that you realize.

What are we to do with our fear? We find the answer in Psalm 34:4:

> I sought the LORD, and He answered me,
> And delivered me from all my fears. (Ps. 34:4)

We must purpose to *seek* God at every point of fear. God uses the temptation to fear to encourage us to seek Him. Seeking God is the pathway to spiritual prosperity. Listen to God's testimony about King Uzziah:

> He continued to seek God in the days of Zechariah, who had understanding through the vision of God; and as long as he sought the LORD, God prospered him. (2 Chron. 26:5)

Seeking God is also the pathway to understanding:

Evil men do not understand justice,
But those who seek the LORD understand all things.
(Prov. 28:5)

There is often deep hurt in our souls, and God desires to give us understanding. It *hurts* to be rejected and this unprocessed hurt in our souls is the grounds for the paralyzing fear of rejection. As we seek God, we can trust Him to put His compassionate healing hand upon the hurts of our souls. We can never fully understand His love for us if we do not experience His understanding of our fears and His willingness to aid us in processing them. His perfect love does cast out fear (1 John 4:18).

As we seek God, we need to trust Him to help *identify* our fears. I was married at age thirty-six and eleven months later He gave us a baby boy. Two and half years later He gave us another boy. I was grateful for our two sons, and as I was approaching my mid-forties, I sensed that our quiver was full. I could tell that my wife did not think so and desired more children. The thought of another child at my age was a very fearful thought. After all, the Bible refers to the "children of one's youth" (Ps. 127:4) and as I did a word study on "youth," I sensed that it was not talking about me!

As I was up in the night praying through this fear, I sensed the need to call the elders of a small church where I had spoken many times throughout the years. I did call one of the elders the next day and asked if he could arrange for the elders to pray over me the next Sunday. He was delighted to honor my request. As they gathered around me and I shared my fear, they all empathized with me and shared their struggles—even a father who had nine children. I did not think he was afraid of anything! After they prayed over me, the tormenting fear was gone. There was a whole new freedom in trusting God in this matter.

One day, a few months later, the Lord met me in His word and prepared me for the day that Penny told me she thought she was pregnant. I rejoiced, and when David, as a small baby, was dedicated to the Lord, I cried as I realized that this baby would not be here apart from the prayers of those elders. God had used them to help me process this fear.

If we *cover* our fear we will *lack* spiritual integrity:

> He who conceals his transgressions will not prosper,
> But he who confesses and forsakes them will find
> compassion. (Prov. 28:13)

When we are seeking God but not talking to Him about our fears, we lack authenticity in our prayers. This type of praying is very tiring. Our inability to process our fears causes us to be fear driven. This was the cause of Saul's sin which cost him his kingship (1 Sam. 15:24).

How is your fear hindering you? In what area of your life is fear paralyzing you and keeping you from opening up to God? Why not let your fears encourage you to seek God, for this is the pathway to true spiritual prosperity and understanding. David, our third son, has been a delight. Isaiah 40:30-31 has been a comfort to me:

Though <u>youths</u> grow weary and tired,
And vigorous <u>young men</u> stumble badly,
Yet those who wait for the LORD
Will gain <u>new strength</u>;
They will mount up with wings like eagles,
They will run and not get tired,
They will walk and not become weary. (Isa. 40:30-31,
emphasis added)

As an older father my instruction is: wait on the Lord!

CHAPTER THIRTY-FIVE

LETTING YOUR FEARS ENCOURAGE YOU TO PURIFY YOUR HEARTS

Why is it that one may cry out to God in prayer and not be heard? Does not God say that "you have not because you ask not" (Jas. 4:2)? What if you ask and you still do not have what you ask for? One possible reason is the problem of double-mindedness. The condition of double-mindedness can open one up to the torment of fear. The opposite of double-mindedness is a pure heart. For that reason James' counsel is to "purify your hearts, you double-minded" (Jas. 4:8).

What is a pure heart? A pure heart is a single heart. The cry of the psalmist is to "unite my heart to *fear* your name" (Ps. 86:11). What does a pure heart look like? We see it expressed in Daniel's life:

> But Daniel made up his mind that he would not defile himself with the king's choice food or with the wine which he drank; so he sought permission from the commander of the officials that he might not defile himself. (Dan. 1:8)

We see it expressed in our Lord's life:

> Jesus said to them, "My food is to do the will of Him who sent Me and to accomplish His work. (John 4:34)

We see it expressed in Paul's life:

> But I do not consider my life of any account as dear to myself, so that I may finish my course and the ministry which I received from the Lord Jesus, to testify solemnly of the gospel of the grace of God. (Acts 20:24)

A pure heart is a heart that has made up its mind to fear and obey God as its greatest priority:

> The man who fears God is described as a "blessed man" (Ps. 112:1), and one of the specific blessings is that "he will not _fear_ bad news" (Ps. 112:7).

For this reason our Lord taught that the fear of God is able to drive out the fear of man:

> Do not fear those who kill the body but are unable to kill the soul; but rather fear Him who is able to destroy both soul and body in hell. (Matt. 10:28)

This truth explains the victory over fear expressed by the psalmist:

> Though a host encamp against me,
> My heart will not fear;
> Though war arise against me,
> In spite of this I shall be confident. (Ps. 27:3)

He was victorious because his heart was pure, as evidenced by this supreme goal in life which he explains in the next verse:

> One thing I have asked from the LORD, that I shall seek:
> That I may dwell in the house of the LORD all the days of my life,
> To behold the beauty of the LORD
> And to meditate in His temple. (Ps. 27:4)

As one seeks God and trusts Him to purify his heart, he will need to *identify* his true goals and motives that may reveal his double-mindedness. A double-minded person is one who is seeking to live for God and something else. Here are some examples:

God and the desire to be popular

We desire to obey God but not to the extent that it may cost us popularity.

God and the desire to get money

We desire to obey God but not to the extent that it may affect our bank account.

God and the desire to be our own boss

We desire to obey God, but we have also determined to not get in a situation where another can tell us what to do. This may arise from having been hurt in the past by someone in authority.

God and the desire to take revenge

We desire to obey God but have reserved for ourselves the right to get even with those who have hurt us.

God and the desire to be sensual

We desire to obey God but fulfilling our sensual appetites outside God's will is an option.

In every case, the other desire becomes the practical *god* of our life. It also opens us up to fear anything that might hinder our fulfilling this desire. For this reason the double-minded person is described in James 1:6-8 as:

- One who doubts and struggles to believe God and experience answered prayer.
- One who is driven and tossed as the wind does the surf of the sea.
- One who is unstable in all his ways.

The double-minded person will struggle to believe God because only the pure in heart can really ascertain the truth about God:

> Blessed are the pure in heart, for they shall see God. (Matt. 5:8)

The double-minded person will be driven and tossed and unstable because he is stripped of his spiritual authority. Only when we are under God's authority do we have spiritual authority:

> Submit therefore to God. Resist the devil and he will flee from you. (Jas. 4:7)

For this reason the next verse confirms the exhortation to purify your hearts, you double-minded (James 4:8).

When one is under God's authority one is able to experience all the dimensions of God's love:

> So that Christ may dwell in your hearts through faith; and that you, being rooted and grounded in love, may be able to comprehend with all the saints what is the breadth and length and height and depth, and to know the love of Christ which surpasses knowledge, that you may be filled up to all the fullness of God. (Eph. 3:17-19)

It is His love that casts out fears (1 John 4:18)! If we cover our fear we will be devoid of eternal fruit because our failure to deal with fear hinders us from abiding in the Lord, and apart from Him we can do nothing of eternal value (John 15:5).

> Unless the LORD builds the house,
> They labor in vain who build it;
> Unless the LORD guards the city,
> The watchman keeps awake in vain.
> It is vain for you to rise up early,
> To retire late,
> To eat the bread of painful labors;
> For He gives to His beloved even in his sleep. (Ps. 127:1-2)

Only what is motivated by love will stand before the judgment seat of Christ (1 Cor. 13:1-3). You will note that fear is behind the sin of pride in Genesis 11:4. One purpose of Christ's death is to free us from living for ourselves that we might live for Him who died and rose again for us (2 Cor. 5:14). It is Christ's liberating death that is the foundation which makes it possible for one to open his life to the Spirit who produces a pure heart of love, enabling him to agree with the cry of the Psalmist:

> Not to us, O Lord, not to us,
> But to your name, give glory[!] (Ps. 115:1)

Our hope is that the Spirit of God who has been sent to honor Christ can fill our hearts and produce in us a desire to honor Christ. Such is the pathway to a life of love that overcomes paralyzing fear.

Let your struggle with fear encourage you to purify your heart. As you seek God, ask Him to identify the goals and motives of your heart. Repent of any wrong goal (see the list in this chapter) and place yourself under God's loving authority. Such is the pathway of "life" and the experience of the grace of prayer and ministry.

CHAPTER THIRTY-SIX

LETTING YOUR FEARS ENCOURAGE YOU TO BELIEVE GOD

The grace of prayer can enable you to transform your fears into faith. As a college student at Auburn University, I surrendered my life to the Lord through the influence of a fraternity brother. Buster had pledged that social fraternity to lead people to Christ. I was fascinated by such a person who took a stand for Christ in the midst of an environment where it was not at all popular to do so. Being his roommate for a year taught me much about the Christian life.

Joining a campus ministry, I had the opportunity to participate in a number of outreach opportunities. I remember one occasion in which a group of us and a Campus Crusade for Christ staff member went to a neighboring town in Alabama and hosted a Christian Living Seminar on Friday night and Saturday. On Sunday we spoke in various churches and Sunday school classes. After giving my testimony of God's blessing to a small group, a dear lady came up to me and voiced these words—"Great suffering is ahead of you." I do not doubt the good intent of this lady or that she was more mature than I at that time. However, the effect of her words was not at all encouraging! I began to fear what might happen. Such a mindset is not of the Lord.

As I noted earlier, the Scripture that God used to dispel this gloom was 2 Corinthians 1:5:

> For just as the sufferings of Christ are ours in abundance, so also our comfort is abundant through Christ.

The assurance that I received that morning was that whatever I experienced, God's comfort would always be sufficient. It would not merely be sufficient for me, but so much that my comfort could even overflow to others (2 Cor. 1:4).

The temptation to fear can be used to encourage us to believe God.[28] This is how Jesus ministered to His fearful and troubled disciples when He told them of His imminent departure from earth:

> Do not let your heart be troubled; believe in God, believe also in Me. (John 14:1)

---

[28] For more on developing faith, see *Living the Life God has Planned: A Guide to Knowing God's Will.* (Chicago, Moody Press, 2001) pp. 56-62.

When we begin to fear what might happen, we begin to be enslaved by fears that could possibly even turn into self-fulfilled prophecies. Proverbs 10:24 even tells us that "what the wicked fears will come upon him." For this reason the psalmist prays for God to preserve his life from the *"dread of the enemy"* (Ps. 64:1). Many times the dread of something is far worse than the actual experience of it. After my eldest son had surgery, a large bandage was across his back. When I tried to remove it, he rejected my attempts with great emotion. This went on for about a week until one night, as he came out of the shower I unexpectedly came up behind him and ripped it off. He said, "That wasn't so bad, Dad!" May God preserve all of us from the dread of what might happen, which may be worse than the event itself.

As we seek God at our points of fear, we need to identify *promises* that answer these fears. This can be a vital step in transforming our fears into faith. When I was asked a number of years ago to speak at a radio program that aired nationwide, I responded by saying that I would pray about it. My real fear was "what if I get on this call-in show and cannot answer the questions?" God illuminated Psalm 67:7 to my spirit, which says that God blesses us that the ends of the earth may fear Him. The principle I derived from this passage gave me the courage to walk through this open door of ministry and God did bless.

After graduating from college and later seminary and a doctoral program, I entered a teaching ministry. I still felt at this time that God wanted me single during these years. I would talk to the Lord about this area of my life. One day while praying, my mind was filled with accusing and condemning words: "You are idealistic. You are not realistic and cannot really trust God to meet your need for companionship!" I felt so low, but at this moment Ephesians 3:20 entered my mind—"Now to Him who is able to do far more abundantly beyond all that we ask or think, according to the power that works within us." This verse silenced those accusing thoughts. For years I stood on this verse and often prayed, "God, I do not know Your will, but I believe you to do above and beyond all I could ask or think." When God sent His woman into my life, it was for me the experience of Ephesians 3:20.

My wife and I were counseled by a godly midwife to seek God for a verse to meditate on during the labor process while giving birth. When my wife's contractions began, I, as a nervous father called the world to pray, only to find out that it was a false alarm. My wife stayed up with some additional minor contractions and also lost all of her food. In this weakened condition the labor did finally begin. It lasted twenty-six hours. God had given her Isaiah 41:10 to lean upon:

> Do not fear, for I am with you;
> Do not anxiously look about you, for I am your God.
> I will strengthen you, surely I will help you,
> Surely I will uphold you with My righteous right hand.

God gave her strength to the very end! Her second labor lasted only six hours, and she said if it had lasted five minutes more she could not have made it. For the third child she called as I was teaching a class. The security guard at our school knocked at my door and told me the news. I was giving an exam and had to collect it—the students were thrilled. I raced home only to find out that the labor had stopped. The next day as I arrived at work and sat down to an important faculty meeting I received word to come home. It was not a word of panic, but I needed to get home. When I arrived, her water had broken and things were moving quickly. Thirty minutes after we arrived at the hospital she gave birth. (A baby just before us had been born in the car, and they named him *Car- son!*) In each case God gave the strength that was needed, and as we looked back at the first birth we marveled at God's faithfulness to the truth of Isaiah 41:10.

God is merciful to come to us in our times of fear and open up His word. I had flown into Chicago to interview for a teaching position at the Moody Bible Institute. The process began by teaching an 8:00 a.m. class before a group of students and four administrators who sat on the back row. It was followed by a series of interviews and appointments that lasted until 5:00. Glancing down at my Bible before I arose to give the morning lecture, I caught the second half of the verse of Psalm 52:1. In the NASB it reads, "The lovingkindness of God endures all day long!" I took it as His invitation to enjoy the day, and it calmed my whole being. It was an enjoyable day, and God opened the door for me to teach at the school.

Our battle with fear should be used to encourage us to believe God. As we seek Him, we are to identify promises to match those fears. You will note that in Appendix Two I have given some examples of this. If we cover our fear, we will lack the *peace* that our wonderful Lord desires to give us:

> Peace I leave with you; My peace I give to you; not as the world gives do I give to you.
>
> Do not let your heart be troubled, nor let it be fearful. (John 14:27)

It is not the will of God that we live in fear of what might happen. The brilliant composer Beethoven lived in constant fear of losing his hearing. His despair was so great that no one could comfort him. The thought of total deafness was painful to him, but his deafness continued to increase. When he realized that God alone could give him the strength to go on, his life took on a new meaning. It was only after complete deafness beset him that he wrote his finest music. Shut out from the distraction of the world, new melody flooded his soul. He came to realize his deafness was a blessing in disguise. Trust in the Lord who is both sovereign and good, and you will experience the grace of prayer and the grace to be a soul physician.

SECTION SEVEN

NEED FOR SPIRITUAL REST—EXPERIENCING THE GRACE OF TRUE PEACE

In order to quench people's thirst for true peace, they need to respond to Jesus' offer to come to Him and drink. He alone can offer a lasting peace which can never be taken away. It can be experienced in any circumstance—even in the midst of the conflicts of life. Jesus called it "rest for your souls."

A soul physician is one who understands the proper place of the spiritual disciplines. He realizes that they can be pursued with the wrong motivations which can hinder his experience of Christ's gracious gifts that He wants him to enjoy. They also can be pursued with the correct goals in mind and become that which the Lord uses to enhance our relationship with Him.

May the following chapters aid you to experience the spiritual rest that can be found only in Christ. May you also be used to point many others to Him in order that they too may experience this rest for their souls as they learn the joy of living under His liberating yoke.

CHAPTER THIRTY-SEVEN

UNDERSTANDING WHAT SPIRITUAL REST IS AND WHAT IT IS NOT

Only the grace of God can lead us into the experience of spiritual rest. After my freshman year in college my *outward* circumstances were very encouraging. I had made the Dean's List every quarter, pledged a social fraternity, been elected President of the School of Business, and received other campus honors. *Inwardly* I was a wreck--full of fear and anxiety. My heart starved for something, and only later would I realize that it was the spiritual *rest* that Christ offers.

What is Spiritual Rest?

It is essential to clearly understand what is meant by spiritual *rest*. Spiritual rest does not mean an end of spiritual conflict in *this life*. The believer is to have the mindset of a *soldier* and should expect life-long warfare. However, there can be *rest now* in the midst of this *warfare*.

The Old Testament speaks of certain spiritual truths in the concrete terms of Israel's experience in the land of Canaan. In the Old Testament, rest is described as a security in knowing that Israel's enemies had been defeated and realizing the enjoyment of their inheritance. For the New Testament Christian, spiritual rest is understanding that Christ's death and resurrection enables the believer to rest securely in the victory He has won over our enemy within ("the flesh") and our enemies without (the world system and the devil). The believer can rest in his inheritance of having been blessed with every spiritual blessing (Eph. 1:3; cf. 1 Pet. 1:3-4). There is certainly to be a rest for believers in the coming kingdom age when Christ reigns and rules supremely (cf. Isa. 32:18; Jer. 50:34) and a rest for the believers in heaven (Rev. 14:13). However, there is also a rest in this life even in the midst of its conflicts. It is a rest where the Lord deals bountifully with our souls (Ps. 116:7).

Who Inquires About Spiritual Rest?

If your soul is inquiring about spiritual rest, it is strong evidence that you have a desire for God's best. You will agree that those who truly desire something will also exhibit a determination to fulfill that desire. Listen to the psalmist express his desire and his determination:

One thing I have asked from the Lord *(His desire)*
That I shall seek *(His determination)*. (Psa. 27:4,
parenthetical comments added by author)

The one who asks the question about spiritual rest has also begun to discover that desire and determination are not enough! They have learned that they cannot live in the strength of their own determination. If you know what it is like to labor, and become weary and burdened down, God may be deepening your desire to ask Him about His rest for your soul.

Who Receives an Answer to Their Inquiry?

There is an often told story of a youth who came to study under a wise man. After this young man expressed his desire to be aided in his knowledge of God, his wise teacher took him to a lake and led him into the water. Without any warning and with his hands on the student's head, he held him under the water. The young man desperately fought his way out of the water to catch his breath. Confused and alarmed his mind sought to find the meaning of this experience. Before he could even ask the question his teacher said, "When you want God as much as you wanted air, you shall find Him."[29]

Our seeking God is merely a response to His seeking us. The one who receives the answer to their question is the one who responds to God's prompting to seek Him. The one

---

[29] S. J. Hill, *Personal Revival* (Pensacola, Florida: Day Spring Publishers, 1999).

who hungers and thirsts for His righteousness is promised satisfaction (Matt. 5:6). Smith Wigglesworth said, "To hunger and thirst after righteousness is when nothing in the world can fascinate us so much as being near to God."[30] God will be found by those who truly seek Him (Matt. 7:7). Anything in your life that is encouraging you to seek God-- thank Him for it! It is the gift of a kind God who wants you to experience the grace of prayer.

One Friday afternoon after having just finished teaching my final class and completing other office responsibilities, in an exhausted state I began to walk to the commuter train that would carry me to my home. As I left my work I sensed an oppressive burden on my heart. My first thought was, "Lord, I'm so tired. Let me just forget about this." However, in response to God's command in Philippians 4:6, I had purposed to seek the Lord at each point of my anxiety. I proceeded to walk into a restaurant and order a cup of hot tea. I took out a sheet of paper and tried to get in touch with what was on my heart. One cup of tea turned out to be seven, and on that Friday afternoon I wrote down some of the most precious insights and convictions that God has ever given me. On the top of the sheet of paper, which I still have, I wrote, "Lord, teach me to see the goodness of every burden that You entrust me with that causes me to seek You."

God entrusts us with fears, anxieties, and hurts in our soul to encourage us to seek Him. As we previously noted the psalmist says, "I sought the Lord . . . and He delivered me from all my fears." (Psa. 34:4) God prompts you to seek

---

[30] W. Hacking, *Smith Wigglesworth Remembered.* (Tulsa, Oklahoma: Harpers House, 1981), 78.

Him that He may spiritually prosper your life. As was said of King Uzziah: "As long as He sought the Lord, God prospered him (2 Chron. 26:5).

The one who seeks the Lord will discover in his experience that there is something more foundational than the determination to do God's will--a continual and complete dependence on God. This can be illustrated in Christ's life and Paul's:

> My food is to do the will of Him who sent me and to accomplish His work. (John 4:34) *(Christ's determination)*

> I can do nothing on my own initiative. As I hear, I judge; and my judgment is just, because I do not seek my own will, but the will of Him who sent me. (John 5:30) *(Christ's dependence)*

> But I do not consider my life at any account as dear to myself, in order that I may finish my course and the ministry which I received from the Lord Jesus, to testify solemnly to the gospel of the grace of God. (Acts 20:24) *(Paul's determination)*

> I have been crucified with Christ; and it is no longer I who live, but Christ who lives in me; and the life which I now live in the flesh I live by faith in the Son of God,

who loved me and gave Himself up for me. (Gal. 2:20) *(Paul's dependence)*

In Chapter twenty-one, we noted the three stages of the Christian life. Eager and enthusiastic promises and resolutions to obey God characterize the first stage. These unfulfilled aspirations lead to the disillusionment and despair of the second stage as one seeks to understand his inability to live out his resolutions in the strength of his dedication. The third stage is characterized by the thought, "Lord, I can't, but I must; and I will trust you to empower me to do it."

We do not pass through these three stages only once! The lesson of dependence has to be learned and relearned many times—each time at a deeper level. If you view spiritual rest as a luxury you need to realize that you have not fully grasped it. It is not a luxury; it is an utter necessity! After you see it in this light, you will come to God and reverently tell Him that for His glory you are not willing to live without it. Now back to Psalm 27:4:

One thing I have asked from the Lord *(His desire),*

That I shall seek *(His determination):*

That I may dwell in the house of the Lord all the days of my life *(His dependence),*

To behold the beauty of the Lord and to meditate in His temple *(His delight).*

(Psa. 27:4, parenthetical comments added by author)

CHAPTER THIRTY-EIGHT

KNOWING THE ONLY SOURCE OF SPIRITUAL REST

The search for spiritual rest can take one in many directions. There is a longing and even a conscious (or unconscious) search for a "spiritual pill" that will enable one to instantly reach spiritual maturity. We may be looking for a certain experience, a conference or seminar, a video series to view, a degree from a school, or any other legitimate means God can use. What we need to realize is the possibility that there may be wrong motives behind this search. In essence we may be looking for something that will enable us to graduate from a life of utter dependence upon the Lord. In God's great compassion for us, He chooses to keep us dependant on Him so that we can experience all the dimensions of His love (cf. Eph. 3:14-19). Christ alone can deliver the promises: "I will give you rest," and "you shall find rest for your souls" (Matt. 11:28-29).

Christ alone is the source of true rest. A lack of spiritual rest is viewed as judgment as seen in Revelation 14:11:

> And the smoke of their torment goes up forever and ever; they have no *rest* day and night, those who worship the beast and his image, and whoever receives the mark of his name. (Rev. 14:11, emphasis added)

Therefore the consistent message of the Scripture is that to resist God's offer of rest is to experience His judgment.

The good news of the gospel is that Jesus Christ bore our judgment to give us every blessing in heaven! He experienced the curse of the agonizing separation from God in order for us to know the promise of His restful presence which can be experienced through the grace of prayer.

Christ --The Revealer of God as the God-man

The grace of prayer is not a mere human activity, but puts us in touch with the true and living God who is revealed in Christ. When the apostle John gave a summary of what he had learned from Christ as an eyewitness and intimate disciple, he stated it this way:

> This is the message we have heard from Him and announce to you, that God is Light, and in Him there is no darkness at all. (1 John 1:5)

Our Lord is the "image of the invisible God" (Col. 1:15). He is the "radiance of [God's] glory and the exact representation of His nature" (Heb. 1:3). He told His disciples that to see Him was to see the very character of the Father because He and the Father were one in essence (John 14:9, 10:30). It is His revelation of God's character that provides the resting place for our faith.[31] The following is a brief summary of God's character:

> He is a **Person.** He made man in his image (Gen. 1:26-27), and He is not simply an impersonal influence but someone *you* can know and trust at all times.
>
> He is a **Spirit.** (John 4:24) You can see the physical world He created, but you can also become acquainted with Him and the spiritual world that He also created. He is able to fill your spirit or God-shaped vacuum and satisfy your deepest longings.
>
> He is **Eternal.** (Psa. 90:2) Your relationship to Him will give a perspective that enables you to view the sufferings of this life differently (Rom. 8:18).
>
> He is **Present Everywhere.** (Psa. 139:7-12) Everywhere you go, He is there. As a believer in Christ this means you always have with you a Father, Friend, Protector and Lover.
>
> He **Knows Everything.** (Psa. 139:1-6) He knows all about your life and your future, and this knowledge

---

[31]For discussion on each aspect of God's character, see: *Living the Life God has Planned: A Guide to Knowing God's Will.* Chicago, Moody Press, 2001, pp. 83-154.

is accompanied by His love. God's will is exactly what you would desire if you knew all the facts.

He is **Wise.** (Jas. 1:5) He is willing and able to give you wisdom to live this life with skill and freedom.

He is **Sovereign.** (1 Chron. 29:11-14) He is the everlasting Ruler, and His purposes will be accomplished. He can even overrule evil for the good of His children (Rom. 8:28).

He is **All-Powerful.** (Rev. 19:6) He can grant you the power to live the beautiful life He created you to live and the power to conquer your fears and anxieties. He is for us and is stronger than our adversaries and displays His power in our weaknesses (Rom. 8:31; 2 Cor. 12:7-10).

He is **Loving.** (Rom. 4:8) He demonstrated His devotion to you by sending Jesus to die for you when you were indifferent and defiant of Him. He desires you to fully experience His love that can cast out your fears (1 John 4:18) and enable you to be more than a conqueror in the most difficult of circumstances (Rom. 8:37). You can rest in His unchanging love (Rom. 8:38-39).

He is **Holy.** (Isa. 6:3) He is totally devoted to what is good and opposed to all actions, attitudes, and words that are against His perfect character. Because of His perfection you can completely trust His heart even when you cannot trace or understand the work of His hands.

He is **Righteous.** (Ps. 9:3-4) No injustice or inequity will be eternally rewarded. God's moral law, which

He has implanted in your conscience, will be eternally vindicated. He will reward every work of faith you do that is prompted by His love (Heb. 6:10, 11:6) even if it seems insignificant or trivial (Mk 9:41).

He is **Faithful and True.** He invites you to entrust your life to Him who alone is perfectly faithful and true. Every morning you can expect to be met by His faithful aid (Lam. 3:23), and you can experience His faithful provision in all your temptations (1 Cor. 10:13) and spiritual conflicts (2 Thess. 3:3). You can also rest in His faithful promise to forgive your sins (1 John 1:9).

He is **Merciful.** He has a deep concern for you in your needs and is able to comfort you in your pain (2 Cor. 1:3) and mercifully renew your spirit to keep you from losing heart (2 Cor. 4:1).

He is **Gracious.** While we deserve His judgment, His grace has provided not only for our salvation from our guilt (Eph. 2:8-9) but also the motivation and power to do anything He requires us to do (1 Cor. 15:10). This is why we refer to the *grace* of prayer in the subtitle of this book.

He is **Good.** (Mk. 10:18) He has an unchanging disposition, generosity, and delight in your eternal welfare. He is the author of *every* good and perfect gift (Jas. 1:17).

He is **Unchanging.** (Mal. 3:6) He is unchanging and unchangeable in all of His beautiful attributes! For example, His love for you is just as intense at this moment as when He was dying on the cross for you. He will never cease to be faithful to you and care for you (Isa. 46:3-4).

The experience of the grace of prayer is a life of trusting this wonderful God!

Christ—The Source of Infinite Spiritual Riches

The grace of prayer and ministry is also experienced as we pray and live in light of our riches in Christ.

Who has the Son?[32]

A Wealthy Art Collector

A wealthy man and his son loved to collect rare works of art. They had everything in their collection, from Picasso to Raphael. They would often sit together and admire the great works of art. When the Vietnam conflict broke out, the son went to war. He was very courageous and died in battle while rescuing another soldier. The father was notified and grieved deeply for his only son.

A Picture of the Son

About a month later, just before Christmas, there was a knock at the door. A young man stood at the door with a large package in his hands. He said, "Sir, you do not know me, but I am the soldier for whom

---

[32] Author unknown, reprinted from public domain.

your son gave his life. He saved many lives that day, and he was carrying me to safety when a bullet struck him in the heart and he died instantly. He often talked about you and your love for art."

The young man held out his package. "I know this is not much. I am not really a great artist, but I think your son would have wanted you to have this." The father opened the package. It was a portrait of his son, painted by the young man. He stared in awe at the way the soldier had captured the personality of his son in the painting. The father was so drawn to the eyes that his own eyes welled up with tears. He thanked the young man and offered to pay for the picture.

"Oh, no sir, I could never repay what your son did for me. It is a gift."

The father hung the portrait over his mantel. Every time visitors came to his home he took them to see the portrait of his son before he showed them any of the other great works he had collected.

Before It Is Given, an Inheritance Always Requires the Death of the Testator

The man died a few months later. There was to be a great auction of his paintings. Many influential people gathered, excited over seeing the great paintings and having an opportunity to purchase one for their own collections. On the platform sat the painting of the son. The auctioneer pounded his gavel.

Auction the Son First

"We start the bidding with this picture of the son. Who will bid for this picture?" There was silence. Then a voice at the back of the room shouted. "We want to see the famous paintings. Skip this one." But the auctioneer persisted. "Will someone bid for this painting? Who will start the bidding? $100, $200?" Another one shouted angrily, "We did not come to see this painting. We came to see the Van Goghs, the Rembrandts. Get on with the real bids!" "The son! The son! Who will take the son?"

I Will Take the Son

Finally, a voice came from the very back of the room. It was the gardener who had long been in the service of the wealthy man whose paintings were being auctioned. "I will give $10 for the painting."

Being a poor man, it was all he could afford. "We have $10; who will bid $20?" "Give it to him for $10. Let us see the masters." "Ten dollars is the bid; won't someone bid $20?" The crowd was becoming angry. They did not want the picture of the son. They wanted the more worthy investments for their collections. The auctioneer pounded the gavel. "Going once, twice, sold for $10!"

A man sitting on the second row shouted, "Now let's get on with the auction!"

He Who Has the Son Has It All

The auctioneer laid down his gavel, "I am sorry, the auction is over." "What about the paintings?" "I am sorry. When I was called to conduct this auction, I was told of a secret stipulation in the will. I was not allowed to reveal that stipulation until this time. Only the painting of the son would be auctioned. Whoever bought that painting would inherit the entire estate, including the other paintings. The one who takes the son gets everything!"

Commitment

Two thousand years ago, God gave His Son to die on a cruel cross. Much like the auctioneer, His message today is, "The Son, the Son, who will take the Son?" Because, you see, whoever takes the Son gets everything.

Christ is not only the perfect revelation of God, but He is also the one who mediates to us every spiritual blessing. In Christ we have every spiritual blessing![33]

> Blessed be the God and Father of our Lord Jesus Christ, who has blessed us with every spiritual blessing in the heavenly places in Christ. (Eph. 1:3)

> Seeing that His divine power has granted to us everything pertaining to life and godliness, through the true knowledge of Him who called us by His own glory and excellence. (2 Pet. 1:3)

---

[33] See Appendix 4

> So then let no one boast in men. For all things belong
> to you, whether Paul or Apollos or Cephas or the world
> or life or death or things present or things to come; all
> things belong to you, and you belong to Christ; and
> Christ belongs to God. (1 Cor. 3:21-23)

The grace of prayer is experienced as your receive His gifts and pray in light of His acceptance and delight (Section One), His hope in your struggles (Section Two), His motivation and enablement (Section Three), His comfort and perspective in your pain (Section Four), His conviction and cleansing (Section Five), His faith in your fears (Section Six), and His rest for your soul (Section Seven).

CHAPTER THIRTY-NINE

BEING TAUGHT BY A GOD OF GRACE

One day during a busy Fall semester, Dr. George Sweeting, the President of Moody Bible Institute at that time, came to the pulpit after the chapel speaker had finished. Dr. Sweeting stunned the audience with these words, "There will be no classes tomorrow. You will come to class but only to pray." With that one announcement, the hours that I had scheduled in order to prepare for my three class lectures were wiped clean. This came as a gift of God, giving all of us added time to seek the Lord and digest the special messages being given in chapel that week.

As I anticipated the next day, I contemplated how to make the most of this opportunity. I talked to the Lord about possibly fasting, but this idea did not seem appropriate for *this* day. I was exhausted and went out for a good breakfast before I got on the train the next morning. Sensing God's leading to even abandon my normal disciplines, I enjoyed being still and quiet before the Lord. It was a day that my body and my spirit received rest. Some spiritual life writers used to refer to a time when we need to "loosen the strings of our bow." My only responsibility was to go to my class and lead in prayer. After saying as few words as I could to introduce the prayer meetings, I prayed along with my classes. I was practically silent most of the day and still before the Lord in my spirit.

As I began to walk home that evening to get on the train, I decided to stop to eat first. I was single at this time and used to frequent a few restaurants. I have often said that they must have thought I died when I got married. That night in this restaurant, a waitress told me something that had never been said to me before. She said it not once or twice but three times. She exclaimed, "I go all over this restaurant and I sense hurry and anxiety, but I come to your booth and I sense peace."

If you had asked me that evening, "What did you do today?" I would have said, "I was still and quiet, spoke very few words, prayed with my classes, and ate good meals." In terms of the world's evaluation it was not a very *productive* day. However, I believe the Lord allowed me to hear the words of the waitress to show me that there is great *fruitfulness* in slowing down and even putting aside one's normal routine of seeking and serving God when He so guides.

A hurried spirit is the death of prayer and grieves and quenches God's Spirit. It is His manifest presence that leads to the provision of rest (cf. Ex. 33:14). As we live under

Christ's yoke, He invites us to "learn from [Him]" (Matt. 11:29). He desires to teach us these unchangeable truths that we have attempted to illuminate in this book which lead to the experience of the grace of prayer and ministry as a soul physician.

We are to look to Him and Him alone as the source of all we need and follow His guidance. He will always honor genuine faith that is willing to cooperate with His plans and avoid the consequences of scheming in unbelief.

> For thus the Lord GOD, the Holy One of Israel, has said,
> "In repentance and rest you will be saved,
> In quietness and trust is your strength."
> But you were not willing,
>
> And you said, "No, for we will flee on horses,"
> Therefore you shall flee!
> "And we will ride on swift horses,"
> Therefore those who pursue you shall be swift.
>
> One thousand will flee at the threat of one man;
> You will flee at the threat of five,
> Until you are left as a flag on a mountain top
> And as a signal on a hill.   (Isa. 30:15-17)

To say that we look to Him always implies a life of faith, but this does not always mean passivity. His leading will not only take into account that you are a spiritual being but that you also live in a physical body. There are times that the most spiritual thing you can do is to get a good night's sleep and eat a good meal. He knows how to refresh each one of us in our unique personalities. There are times that we do need to get away from the normal demands of life just as our Lord instructed His disciples to do on one occasion:

> And He said to them, "Come away by yourselves to a secluded place and rest a while." (For there were many people coming and going, and they did not even have time to eat.)
> (Mark 6:31)

There are times that our rest can be found in the gracious provision of godly fellowship as the apostle Paul prayed to find refreshing rest in the company of the church of Rome (Rom. 15:32). The Lord is our Shepherd and He knows how to cause us to lie down in green pastures and beside quiet waters (Psa. 23:2). The Hebrew verbs in Psalm 23:2 are in a causative stem which imply His provisions of rest stem from His initiative rather than from our initiative. I like God's description of the home of a righteous man--it is referred to as a "resting place" (Prov. 24:15).

The Place of Discipline

I have continually referred to the grace of prayer and how it leads to spiritual rest. You might rightly ask, "How do the concepts of discipline and grace fit together?" I have focused on the spiritual discipline of prayer and ministry. Other disciplines such as study, service, fellowship, and witnessing are important. However, all the disciplines must be inserted into the framework of God's grace.

Wrong Motivations for the Spiritual Disciplines

How do you know if you are approaching prayer or any discipline in a way that is not consistent with God's grace?

You do not approach the spiritual disciplines in order to be accepted by God. This is the message of Section One, chapters one to twelve of this book.

You do not approach the spiritual disciplines in order to have victory over sin. Unquestionably, God uses the disciplines to aid us in our struggle, but the danger is to try to make something *we do* the foundation rather than what the Lord has done! This is the message of Section Two, chapters thirteen to eighteen of this book.

You do not approach the spiritual disciplines to gain motivation in the Christian life. There is some truth in the fact that our participation in the disciplines does motivate us, but the error is in changing our object of trust from Christ and His *devotion* to us, to ourselves and our devotion to Him. We are to look to Christ alone to provide the motivation and power to live the Christian life and let Him guide us to the discipline that He uses as means of His grace. This is the message of Section Three, chapters nineteen to twenty-two of this book.

You do not approach the spiritual disciplines in order to get cleansing from the guilt of your sin. As we mentioned, we need to be aware of guilt motivations in our lives that produce dead works. This is the message of Section Five, chapters thirty to thirty-three of this book.

Correct Goals of the Spiritual Disciplines

The spiritual disciplines are glorious and gracious provisions of God. The problem is when we begin to look to them in a way that detracts from Christ and His finished work. Our motivation and enablement to live the Christian life, our authority to live the Christian life, our acceptance, and the provision of cleansing and restoration are found in CHRIST and CHRIST alone.

God certainly uses the spiritual disciplines to aid us in becoming like Christ. They are tools (which are indicators of our spiritual maturity), that the Spirit of God can use to aid us in becoming conformed to Christ's image rather than ends in themselves.

Spiritual disciplines are needed to strengthen our spirits. When we read the one-verse summary of how John the Baptist matured, we read that he become strong in spirit (Luke 1:80). The same is said of our Lord's human development (see Luke 2:40). Every person God has created has been given a spirit. When a person becomes a Christian his spirit is made alive so that he can have a relationship with God. This is called regeneration. As we grow, God desires that we become strong in our spirit rather than in our fleshly drives. For this reason Paul prays for the believers in Ephesus to be strengthened (same Greek word as in Luke 1:80 and 2:40) in their inner man (or human spirit) by the Holy Spirit (Eph. 3:16). As we engage in the spiritual disciplines we are cooperating with the Spirit (cf. Gal. 6:8—sow to the Spirit).

Spiritual disciplines are means that we can use to better *know* Christ and the riches we have in Him. In that way we can mature in knowing His love for us and respond to this love by loving Him with all our being which is the greatest goal in all of life (Matt. 22:37-39).

Spiritual disciplines are also a means that God uses to cause us to pursue godliness (1 Tim. 4:7). In practical terms, godliness is becoming like God in His moral character as we occupy ourselves with Him and practice His presence. Spiritual disciplines are wonderful provisions of God. As you pursue them, be sure to *continue* in the *grace* of God!

Dick Averbeck has been a leader in promoting spiritual transformation in the training of leaders for the next generation. He likens the Holy Spirit to the wind and the believer to a boat. In this analogy the spiritual disciplines are the sail that one raises to catch the winds, just as the various spiritual disciplines need to be directed and energized by the Spirit. The Spirit of God will prompt you to get your sails up and receive His enablement in becoming a Christ-like person, engaging in meaningful fellowship with others and doing your part in sharing the grace of God with God's people and with His lost world.

It is my prayer that every reader of this book will continue to grow in the disciplines, as they are pursued within the context of God's grace, and experience true rest.

CHAPTER FORTY

KNOWING THE PLACE TO EXPERIENCE SPIRITUAL REST

The grace of God leads to the place of rest because it allows us to maintain fellowship with Christ and live under His liberating yoke.

> Come to Me, all who are weary and heavy-laden, and I will give you rest. Take My yoke upon you and learn from Me, for I am gentle and humble in heart, and YOU WILL FIND REST FOR YOUR SOULS. For My yoke is easy and My burden is light. (Matt. 11:28-30)

Jesus tells us that there is only one place to experience rest—under His yoke (Matt. 11:29). He was speaking to a people who were under the load of their own sin and guilt. His invitation to all men is to exchange this burden for the gift of His yoke. Dr. Dwight Pentecost describes the agricultural background of this metaphor:

> On Sunday afternoon I used to go out to a little rural Sunday school to teach. One afternoon the superintendent of the Sunday school, a farmer, and I were visiting in the community. There was an old farmer plowing with a team of oxen. As I saw this team I was somewhat amazed, for one was a huge ox and the other a very small bullock. That ox towered over the little bullock that was sharing the work with him. I was amazed and perplexed to see a farmer trying to plow with two such unequal animals in the yoke and commented on the inequality to the man with whom I was riding. He stopped his car and said, "I want you to notice something. See the way those traces are hooked to the yoke? You will observe that the large ox is pulling all the weight. That little bullock is being broken in to the yoke but he is not actually pulling any weight." My mind instinctively came to this passage of Scripture where our Lord said, "Take my yoke upon you and learn from me, for I am gentle and humble in heart, and you will find rest for your souls."
>
> In the normal yoke the load is equally distributed between the two that are yoked together, but when we are yoked with Jesus Christ, He bears the load and we who are yoked with Him share in the joy and the accomplishment of the labor but without the

burden of the yoke. The tragedy is that some of us have never been broken into the yoke.[34]

To be able to live under Christ's yoke is a gift. He says that His yoke is easy to wear and that His load is light. A Scripture that may seem far removed from you is the verse, "There is no peace for the wicked" (Isa. 48:22). Our reply is, "Yes, they do not deserve rest and peace." Let us ask ourselves one simple question, "What is more wicked than telling the Lord that He cannot rule over a certain area of our life?" Such refusal to live under Christ's yoke robs us of a life of rest and peace.

I can still remember the thoughts that went through my mind during a meeting when the speaker was encouraging the people to surrender their lives to the Lord. My sad, erroneous thought was, "I wonder what unlucky person will get caught tonight. I guess somebody has to do it, but I feel sorry for them." I obviously did not know God. If God is perfectly loving and perfectly wise, and it is possible to live under His control, would it not be insane not to do so? Yes, and sin is insane! To sin against God is to injure oneself (Prov. 8:35-36).

When I begin to see Christ's offer of His yoke as a *gift*, I also begin to understand God's loving discipline of His children. When Israel rejected His rule, He disciplined them by letting them live under the cruel rule of the Babylonians and the Assyrians. If we refuse Christ's rule He will permit us to live under the rule of our own deceitful desires and under the rule of the opinions of people. Christ died to free

---

[34] Dwight Pentecost, "Out of Bondage", *Kindred Spirit,* Fall 1986, p. 10.

us from the bondage of living to please ourselves and please the world and to experience the liberty of His loving yoke. I remember the person who said he had learned what "BUSY" stood for—"**B**eing **U**nder **S**atan's **Y**oke." Why not tell the Lord that your greatest desire is to let Him control your life?

I heard Dr. Carl Armerding speak when he was eighty-five years old. He shared how he had come to Christ at the age of 15. At age 17 he read Romans 12:1 which says, "I urge you therefore, brethren, by the mercies of God, to present your bodies a living and holy sacrifice, acceptable to God, which is your spiritual service of worship." This verse struck him and he asked a fellow Christian if he had ever read it. "Oh, sure, I've memorized it," was his reply. "Have you ever done it?" he inquired. "No." "Do you know how?" "No." He then asked another who said, "Go to your room and lock the door, get on your knees, put your finger on the text, and tell God you want to do it." So as he followed this instruction, he explained how God illuminated his mind, showing him that He meant everything—every part of his body was to be presented to Him. He made this spiritual transaction before leaving his room that day and now was talking about it almost seventy years later. "This transaction has saved me and preserved me from all kinds of sin and has made countless decisions for me in these last seventy years," he exclaimed. He has found rest under the yoke of Jesus.

Fear is probably the biggest enemy to fully surrendering the control of one's life to the Lord. That God will never abandon us (Heb. 13:5), is not the only thing we need to know, but also that He asks us to abandon ourselves to Him.

Is there any area of your life, any relationship or any possession of which Christ does not have complete access and control? Why not ask God what it is going to cost you to hang on to it? Is it not as foolish as Esau selling his birthright for a bowl of stew? In the authority of Christ, release your grip on it and surrender it to Christ. Let Him remind you that His will is "exactly what you would desire if you knew all the facts." I thank God for the things He has provided for me for which I would never have known how to ask. I also praise Him for the things He has *withheld,* that I craved at one time. He is a wise and loving God, so let this love cast out your fears.

The following prayer is something I wrote down after hearing a tape by Dr. Charles Stanley on the yielded life. Perhaps these words express the desire of your heart:

> Based on a right view of You and all that You have done for me in Christ, I joyfully make a definite commitment that I recognize Your ownership of my life. I yield every part of my life and all my possessions and relationships for Your possession and control from this moment forth and forever, I am available for whatever You want, wherever You want it, and however You want it as long as I live. All my decisions will be based on this. I trust You and You alone to maintain this commitment.

> For Your glory and my eternal benefit. Amen.

Our presenting of ourselves to Him is only a response to the revelation of His merciful character and the infinite riches that He has provided for us in Christ (Rom. 12:1; Eph. 1:3). One day I read a sermon that told the story of a missionary in the Belgian Congo who saw a native being attacked by a lion. He shot the lion, took the native home, and nursed him to health. The injured man was then able to return to his own home. One day the native returned with his wife, his children, a few pigs, and some chickens. He knelt down before the missionary, "Sir, it is the law of my tribe and the law of the forest that if a man has saved your life from a lion, you and all that you have belongs to that man. Here I am. Have all of my possessions. I am your slave." It is Christ who not only has saved us and fully accepts us, but also makes it possible to present ourselves and all of our members to Him! Open your life completely to His love, and He will allow you to experience His grace—the grace that alone will enable you to be all that He created you to be.

God will take care of what is presented to Him. Over thirty years ago I received a letter that contained the following illustration. It said if you owned a house and the roof caved in, you would have a problem. However, if you sold the house to another and the roof caved in, someone else would have a problem. In reverence to God, when you have presented your life to Him, your problems are His problems. He is able to guard what is entrusted to Him (2 Tim. 1:12). It is reassuring to tell God at a moment when you may be confused and in need of guidance, "Lord, my life and all the days of my life are in Your hands. It is up to You to put me in the place where You can receive the greatest glory. Where You lead, I will follow."

As you abandon yourself to Him, He will never abandon you—not ever. His grace will be sufficient, for he pours it out upon the humble (Jas. 4:6). When Polycarp was given the opportunity to swear His allegiance to Caesar and denounce Christ in order to be spared from being burned at the stake, he replied, "Eighty and six years have I served Him and He never did me wrong, how then can I blaspheme my King who saved me?"

May each of us experience this grace and keep crying out to the Lord until He takes us home to be with Him.

APPENDIX ONE

VERSES TO AID ONE IN THE STRUGGLE WITH GUILT

Verses That Aid in One's View of God

Psalm 86:5	God is "ready to forgive" a repentant heart.
Proverbs 28:13	God is merciful to one who confesses and forsakes one's sin.
Romans 8:1	God does not condemn a true believer to the penalty or power of sin.
Romans 8:31	God is for the believer.

Romans   God's love is constant for the believer.
8:38-39

Verses That Aid One's Understanding of Christ's Death

John 19:30   "It is finished" was our Lord's cry on the
               cross which carries the idea that the debt for
               our sin was paid in full.

1 John 2:2   Christ's death fully satisfied God's wrath so
               that He is righteously free to deal with us in
               kindness. This Godward side of the cross is
               called "propitiation."

Verses That Aid One in Understanding Forgiveness

Psalm   Note the completeness of God's removal of
103:12   one's sin.

Psalm 130:3-   The result of understanding one's
4   forgiveness is a proper fear of God.

Isaiah 43:25   God's forgiveness for His name's sake in
                that He glorifies His gracious, merciful, and
                loving character.

Ezekiel 36:25   God cleanses us from all filthiness and
                idolatry as a provision of the new covenant.

Micah 7:19   God takes our sins and casts them into the
                depths of the sea. Corrie ten Boom used to
                say that He also puts up a sign that says,
                "No fishing."

Colossians   God forgives *all* of our sins.
2:13-14

Hebrews   God says He will remember our sins no
10:17   more.

Verses That Show the Need of a Clear Conscience

1 Timothy 1:18-19

1 Peter 3:16

Verses That Give Promises to a Believer Who Confesses His Sin

Proverbs 28:13

1 John 1:7; 9

Verses That Show God's Desire to Restore a Believer to the Blessing of Being under His Authority

James 4:6-10

Verses That Aid in Dealing with the Memory of One's Past

John 4:13-14	Jesus offers forgiveness to one who had had five husbands and was presently living in immorality with one who was not her husband. She becomes a witness to the whole city.
Luke 7:44-50	Jesus forgives an immoral woman and states that an understanding of forgiveness produces a greater love for God.
2 Chronicle 16:9	We cannot offer God a heart that has never sinned, but we can offer Him a whole heart that trusts Him alone.

1 Corinthians 15:8-10	Paul credits God's grace for his life and his call to ministry. He states that this same grace even enabled him, the least of all the apostles, to labor more than all of the apostles.
1 Timothy 1:12-17	Paul credits God's mercy for saving him who was the chief of sinners, a blasphemer, a persecutor, and a violent aggressor. This mercy and perfect patience toward him was to provide the hope that anyone can be saved.
Romans 8:28-29	To the repentant heart, God is able to *work together* that which was not good—even one's sin—into that which can conform us to Christ's image.

APPENDIX TWO

EXAMPLES OF SCRIPTURE THAT ANSWER OUR FEARS

The Fear of Opposition

Romans
8:31

Realize there is One who is for you.

The Fear of Failure

Realize that true success is obeying God and doing His will. The pattern of success is seen in John 17:4:

> I glorified You on the earth, having accomplished the work which You have given Me to do.

In any situation you are a success if you trust Christ to be honored and God to accomplish His purpose (cf. Phil. 1:20).

The Fear of Harm from Evil

Psalm 121:7-8	The Lord is our Protector.
Proverb 12:21	No real (eternal) harm can befall the righteous.
Romans 8:28	God overrules evil for good.

The Fear of Rejection

Psalm 27:10	Even if one is rejected by a father or mother, he can still walk into the welcoming arms of the Lord.

The Fear of Old Age

Psalm 92:14-15	One can still bear fruit in old age.
Isaiah 46:3-4	God will be unchangingly faithful to us from birth to old age.

The Fear of Loneliness

| Hebrews 13:5 | Christ will never leave us or forsake us. |

APPENDIX THREE

(Summary of Chapters 34-36)

We are to admit our fears--not cover or deny them.

What happens when you ADMIT?		What happens when you COVER?
1. Encourages you to see God. (Psa. 34:4)	1. Identify your fear.	1. Lack spiritual integrity and become fear driven. (Psa. 28:13; 1 Sam. 15:24)
2. Encourages you to purify your hearts. (Jas. 4:8)	2. Identify your goals and motives.	2. Lack eternal fruit. (Prov. 127:1-2; John 15:5)
3. Encourages you to believe God. (John 14:1)	3. Identify promises.	3. Lack peace. (John 14:27)

APPENDIX FOUR

UNDERSTANDING OUR SPIRITUAL RICHES

As a *start* to understanding your spiritual riches look at these four passages and observe the blessings that belong to *you*. As a believer in Christ you can say:

Romans 5:

1. God has declared me righteous (Rom. 5:11; 8:30).
2. I have peace with God (Rom. 5:11).
3. I stand in God's grace (Rom. 5:2 cf. Heb. 5:4:16).
4. I have a glorious future hope of experiencing His glory (Rom. 5:2).
5. I can have a new attitude toward trials, knowing that they are for my good (Rom. 4:3-5; 8:28).
6. I have been given the Holy Spirit (Rom. 5:5; 8:9).
7. I have a hope that will not disappoint (Rom. 3:5).
8. I am loved even when I was helpless, ungodly and a sinner (Rom. 5:6-8).
9. I have assurance of salvation from future wrath (Rom. 5:9).

10.   I have been reconciled to God (Rom. 5:11).

Romans 6:

1.   I have died to sin's control over my life and can live a
      new life (Rom. 6:1-10).
2.   I have been freed to present every member of my
      body to God that they may be instruments of
      righteousness (Rom. 6:11-14).
3.   I have been "freed" from a slavery to sin and am a
      slave of righteousness and a slave of God (Rom.
      6:15-23).

Romans 8:

1.   I am not condemned to the penalty or power of sin
      (Rom. 8:1).
2.   I have the Spirit of God and belong to Him (Rom.
      8:9).
3.   My spirit has been made alive to God (Rom. 8:10).
4.   I have the Holy Spirit who leads me into freedom,
      intimacy with God, assurance and hope (Rom. 8:14-
      17).
5.   I am a heir of God and a fellow-heir with Christ
      (Rom. 8:17)
6.   I have a glorious future (Rom. 8:18).
7.   I have the hope of a redeemed body (Rom. 8:23).

8.   I have the Holy Spirit to communicate my deepest longings to God even when I do not know how to express them (Rom. 8:26-27).
9.   I have a God who rules the world and overrules every event under heaven for my eternal good (Rom. 8:28).
10.   I have been chosen by God (Rom. 8:29; Eph. 1:4).
11.   I have been predestined to be conformed to the image of Christ (Rom. 8:29).
12.   I have been called into a relationship with Christ (Rom. 8:30).
13.   I have the absolute assurance of being glorified (Rom. 8:30).
14.   God is for me and greater than all my opposition (Rom. 8:31).
15.   I have been given the gift of Christ and will never lack anything I need to do His will (Rom. 8:32).
16.   I have a Savior who is praying for me at all times (Rom. 8:34; cf. Heb. 7:25).
17.   I can overwhelmingly conquer in all circumstances (Rom. 8:37).
18.   I can never be separated from God's love (Rom. 8:38-39).

Ephesians 1:3-14

1.   I have been chosen by God (Eph. 1:4)
2.   I have been predestined to enjoy the full rights of being adopted into God's family (Eph. 1:5)
3.   I have been freely favored with God's grace (Eph. 1:6, 8)

4.   I have been redeemed by Christ's blood (Eph. 1:7)
5.   I have been fully forgiven of all my sins (Eph. 1:7)
6.   I have received the revelation of God's purpose that
        one day every knew will bow to Christ (Eph. 1:9-10;
        cf. Phil. 2:4-11)
7.   I have been given a glorious inheritance and am so
        esteemed by God that He calls me His inheritance
        (Eph. 1:11, 18)
8.   I have been sealed with the Spirit (Eph. 1:13)

Now as you read the New Testament add to this!!!

ARE YOU WORSHIPPING *THE* GOD OF GRACE?

✝ Do you thank Him for *every* good and perfect gift realizing that anything you receive, other than His eternal wrath, is due to His grace? (Jas. 1:17)

✝ Do you realize that Christ's work has set you free from the condemnation of not measuring up and has enabled you to be fully accepted as God's beloved child? (Rom. 8:1)

✝ Do you realize that Christ's work has set you free from the bondage of your spiritual enemies—your flesh, the world system, and the devil and his demonic spirits? (Gal. 2:20, 6:14; Col. 2:15)

✝ Do you realize that you are asked to rest in God and let Him produce a life that honors Himself, benefits others, and gives you fulfillment? (John 15:5)

✝ Do you realize that all prideful boasting is sin? (1 Cor. 1:30)

✟ Do you realize that you are not the ultimate judge of anyone but there is only One judge? (Jas. 4:12)

✟ Do you seek to affirm others in every way you can, value the dignity of other people, and support and encourage others with your words and in your style of leadership? (Eph. 4:29; 1 Pet. 5:1-3)

✟ Do you realize that God will give you the motivation and enablement to live out every command of the Scripture and face every challenge in life? (2 Cor. 12:7-10; 1 Cor. 15:10)

✟ Do you realize that living under grace does not imply that there are no consequences for sin, but it does imply that there is forgiveness and that God is able to weave your past failure into his plan and bless a repentant heart? (Rom. 8:29)

✟ Are you willing to be misunderstood (Rom. 6:1) or even persecuted because of your understanding of grace? (Gal. 4:21-31)

Study Guide for *How to Be a Soul Physician:*

Learning How Christ Meets the Deepest Longings of a Soul through the Grace of Prayer

Week One

SECTION 1 – Chapters 1-6

Day One – Read chapters 1-2 and respond to the following questions:

- Have you praised God today because He is continually thinking of you (Ps. 139:17-18)? If not, write out your praise to Him right now.
- Read the quotes by S.J. Hill and Ravi Zacharias. Pray that God would overwhelm you with His love for you. Write out your prayer.
- Read the gospel analogy in the beginning of chapter 2. Do you see yourself as a child of the King or as a pathetic beggar in the street? Ask God to expose any wrong thinking of yourself.
  - ○ Do you see yourself as one in whom God delights or are you trying to earn this (Ps 18:19)?
  - ○ Do you see yourself as perfectly justified in God's sight or as a failure before Him (Rom. 5:1)?
  - ○ Do you see yourself as perpetually reconciled or do you fear His rejection (Rom. 5:10)?
  - ○ Do you praise God that Christ bore your wrath and is your propitiatory sacrifice (Rom. 3:25)?
- Meditate on the story of the Korean pastor and write out your praise that God is your Heavenly Father who adopted you into His family.

Day Two – Read chapter 3 and respond to the following questions:

- Is your first instinct when you are in trouble to call upon your Heavenly Father?
- Take time to ponder your heritage through the eyes of a sovereign and good God. How did God use your experience with your parents to prepare you to know Him as the one perfect Father?

Day Three – Read chapter 4 and respond to the following questions:

- Carefully read through the Scriptural truths of what God says about you. Of the ones that are listed write down three of them that are the most precious to you at this time.
- In faith pray the prayer at the end of the chapter.

Day Four – Read chapters 5-6 and respond to the following questions:

- Review the story of Tom coming boldly to the throne of grace. With what concern do you need to come with freedom to the throne of grace right now?
- What did Mishna understand about Jesus that made Him different?
- In what situation can you most rejoice because Christ understands you and will never desert you nor forsake you (Heb. 13:5)?

Week Two

SECTION 1 – Chapters 7-12

Day One – Read chapter 7 and respond to the following questions:

- What is the one time that God is portrayed as being in a hurry?
- How does Romans 8:28 comfort a repentant heart in regard to past sin?
- How do the words of James 4:8 show you God's reconciling heart (cf. James 4:4 to see to whom he is speaking) (cf. Prov. 28:13)?

Day Two – Read chapter 8 and respond to the following questions:

- Prayerfully read 1 Cor. 9:19 and ask God in the authority of Christ to lead you into the full experience of freedom that enables you to be a servant.
- Write down one example in your life where you need to experience being free from the lordship of the expectations of others.
- Write down one example in your life where you need to experience being free from letting the responses of others be the basis of your joy in the Lord.

Day Three – Read chapters 9-10 and respond to the following questions:

- Pray through the list that describes the differences between false and true service. Write down one contrast that is most noticeable to you.
- In response to the last paragraph of Chapter 9, write out your prayer to God believing Him to lead you in the freedom of living before God.
- As you read chapter 9, ask God to show you one specific way your relationships could benefit from living under Christ's control. Write this down and believe God for it.
- Read chapter 10 and ask God to overwhelm you with His love and acceptance!

Day Four – Read chapters 11-12 and respond to the following questions:

- How do you think the story of Luke 10:38-42 relates to the preceeding story of the Good Samaritan (10:25-37) and the following passage on prayer (11:1-13)?
- In your ambition to lead a restful life (1 Thess. 4:11), what care or burden do you need to cast on the Lord right now (Phil. 4:6-7)?
- What is the difference between giving mental assent to the truth of God's acceptance for you and resting in this truth?

Week Three

SECTION 2 – Chapters 13-18

Day One – Read chapter 13 and respond to the following questions:

- Of which expressions of the self-life or flesh are you most conscious?
- What is the problem with making our desire, determination, or discipline the foundation for a victorious life?
- What is the only appropriate foundation?
- What experience has God given to each of us to prepare us to understand the truth of being "in Christ"?
- What does it mean to have "died to sin"?
- Give an illustration of this concept.

Day Two – Read chapters 14-15 and respond to the following questions:

- Write out your explanation of the meaning of the command of Romans 6:11.
- What insight do you gain from the illustration of the covey of quail?
- What insight do you gain from the illustration about the eagle and the prairie chickens?
- Write down the greatest battle in your life in regard to your struggle with sin. Thank God for the truth of Romans 6:11 in relation to this struggle.

Day Three – Read chapter 16 and respond to the following
questions:

- Read the illustration of how they catch monkeys in
  North Africa. On what person, possession, or
  position is it most difficult for you to release your
  grip?
- What do these verses teach us about sin?
  o Hebrews 3:13
  o Proverbs 8:36
  o Jeremiah 5:25
- Would you write down your cry to God for
  deliverance from the deceit of sin?

Day Four – Read chapters 17-18 and respond to the
following questions:

- Write down one of your greatest struggles. Write
  down your praise of Christ for dying and rising again
  to give you victory in this area.
- Ask God to show you the root cause of this struggle
  which you just wrote out and write out your insight.
- Pray for yourself and at least one other person so
  that God would give you "hope" in your greatest
  struggle (see Eph. 1:15-23).
- Look at the words that inspired D.L. Moody to
  consecrate himself to the Lord. Meditate on Romans
  6:11-13 and write out your own prayer of full
  consecration to the Lord.

Week Four

SECTION 3 – Chapters 19-22

Day one – Read chapter 19 and respond to the following questions:

- Prayerfully read 1 Peter 5:2 and ask God if anything is quenching a "want to" motivation to pray. Write out what God shows you.
- Define "grace" in I Corinthians 15:10. How can you relate it to the truth of Ezekiel 36:27?
- Can you believe God to keep you faithful to Him and to cause you to persevere to the end of your life? What encouragement do you get from these verses? Write out your response to each verse.
  - Philippians 2:13
  - Romans 15:5
  - Lamentations 3:23

Day Two – Read chapter 20 and respond to the following questions:

- How does Colossians 1:29 put together "our" role and God's role in the Christian life?
- How does every command of God contain a hidden promise when you understand God's grace?
- Will you come right now to God and humbly ask Him for the grace of prayer? Write out your prayer response.

Day Three – Read chapter 21 and respond to the following questions:

- Who is the Holy Spirit?
- Why is it absolutely necessary to depend on the Holy Spirit to live the Christian life?
- Explain the three stages of the Christian life.
- Examine your life by the following three questions and note any insight that comes to your mind.
  - Am I open to God's Control?
  - Am I trusting God's control?
  - Am I responding to God's control?
- In your own words answer the question, "How can I be filled with the Spirit?"

Day Four – Read chapter 22 and respond to the following questions:

- What does it mean to come boldly to the throne of grace (Hebrews 4:16)?
- What do you need to boldly talk to God about right now? Write out your prayers.
- What is a "point of pride"? Would you ask God to show you any points of pride in your life right now (James 4:6)? Write down any insight you gain.
- How do "thorns" enable you to experience "greater grace" (II Corinthians 12:7-10, James 4:6)?
- What thorn has God used or is He currently using in your life?

Week Five

SECTION 4 – Chapters 23-29

Day One – Read chapter 23-24 and respond to the following questions:

- What is one of the most challenging difficulties with which you need God's understanding, comfort, and healing touch? Prayerfully read chapter 23 and talk to the Lord about this difficulty.
- Prayerfully Read chapter 24 with the difficulty in mind and ask Him to help you put it in the perspective of eternity (read Romans 8:28 and 2 Cor. 4:17-18).
- Come boldly to His throne of grace and tell Him you desire His healing touch upon the pain of your soul in a way that glorifies Him. Take personal responsibility for any disobedience on your part and accept His cleansing blood (cf. John 1:9). Praise Him in faith for the good that He can bring out of your pain.

Day Two – Read chapter 25 and respond to the following questions:

- Do you have any "dread" in your life—something you fear might happen? Prayerfully read 2 Corinthians 1:5 and I Peter 3:13-14 and write down the comfort they give.
- Think of a past or present trial in your life. Process it by stating how it has or is enabling you to: Know God

- As "Father of mercies" (Carefully look at the Scriptures listed under this heading.)
- As "God of all comfort"
  o Learn to lean on God
  o Enhance your ministry

Day Three – Read chapters 26-27 and respond to the following questions:

- What are some of the active or passive ways that you express your anger?
- Could you be described as a "teacup" or a "barrel"?
- Think of a situation in which you have been hurt. What are some reasons why we do not want to forgive the one who hurt us? (We know they are wrong but write them out.)
- In chapter 27, pray through a situation where you need to forgive someone. Which of the consequences of not forgiving gives you greater motivation to obey God?

Day Four – Read chapters 28-29 and respond to the following questions:

- How was Corrie ten Boom able to forgive the guard who abused and killed her sister?
- What is the proper way to view one who has hurt you?
- How does praising God for His forgiveness aid us in forgiving others?
- In an area of repeated failure, ask God in the authority of Christ's shed blood to build a new

pattern of thinking and response. Write down your
prayer.

- What does it mean to truly forgive a person?
- As you read chapter 29, ask God to show you if you
  are wrongly placing a demand on Him, others, or
  yourself. Write down any insight. Also ask Him for
  the wisdom to yield this desire or need to the Lord.

Week Six

SECTION 5 – Chapters 30-33

Day One – Read chapter 30 and respond to the following questions:

- What are some wrong ways that one can respond to guilt? With which of these can you most readily identify?
- How does God's conviction differ from condemnation?
- Think of an area in which God is convicting you. What are three things that He is saying to you according to chapter 30?

Day Two – Read chapter 31 and respond to the following questions:

- Meditate on 1 John 1:5 and write down a prayer of praise for the truth in this verse.
- Why was Jesus the most joyous person who ever lived (Heb. 1:9)?
- Explain what needs to be absent to walk in fellowship with God (I John 1:6,8,10)
- Explain in your own words what it means to walk in the light. Are you and God in agreement at this moment? If you answered "no" to the previous question, what would you need to do to answer "yes"?

Day Three – Read chapter 32 and respond to the following
questions:

- Look at the differences between the Spirit's
  Convictions and the Adversary's Accusations. Which
  contrasts are the most helpful to you?
- With what example of false guilt can you most
  readily identify?

Day Four – Read chapter 33 and answer the following
questions:

- Define a "clear conscience."
- What are some negative consequences of not having
  a clear conscience?
- Prayerfully read chapter 33 and ask the Lord to
  search your heart for any area in which you lack the
  inward assurance of a clear conscience before God.
  Lay this matter before God. Be willing to follow any
  advice He would give and trust Him to be able to put
  your head on the pillow of your bed tonight with a
  clear conscience.
- Prayerfully look at Appendix One and write down
  the verses which are a special aid to you.

Week Seven

SECTION 6 – Chapters 34-36

Day One - Read chapter 34 and respond to the following questions:

- Explain the difference between the purifying fear of the Lord and paralyzing fears.
- How does fear hinder a husband or wife in obeying God's instructions in their marriage roles?
- What specific fear in your life is encouraging you to seek God?
- What promise is given to one who seeks God (2 Chron. 26:5, Prov. 28:5)?

Day Two – Read chapter 35 and respond to the following questions:

- Define a "pure heart." Give Scriptural examples of a pure heart.
- Define double-mindedness.
- Note the five examples of double-mindedness given in this chapter and ask God to show you if one of these characterizes your life. Write down any insight you get.
- What are the consequences of double-mindedness according to James 1:6-8?

Day Three – Reread chapter 35 and ask God to search your heart today and to give you the grace of repentance of any area of double-mindedness. Write down any work God does in your life.

Day Four – Read chapter 36 and think of an area in your life in which you are prone to fear. Ask God to lead you to a specific promise that answers this fear. Write down the fear and the promise. You may find help in Appendix Two.

Week Eight

SECTION 7 – Chapters 37–40

Day One - Read chapter 37 and respond to the following questions:

- What is spiritual rest?
- Who inquires about spiritual rest?
- Who gets their question answered?

Day Two – Read chapter 38 and respond to the following questions:

- Jesus is the only source of spiritual rest (Matt. 11:28-29). He is the revealer of God. Take time to worship and praise God for the attributes of God that are listed in this chapter.
- Meditate on the truth of Ephesians 1:3, 2 Peter 1:3, and II Corinthians 1:3. Look through Appendix 4 and note five things that stand out to you.

Day Three – Read chapter 39 and respond to the following questions:

- List the four wrong motivations for the spiritual disciplines.
- Write down three correct goals for the spiritual disciplines.

Day Four – Read chapter 40 and respond to the following questions:

- What is the place where one can experience spiritual rest?
- Do you view Christ's yoke as a gift?
- Would you be willing to follow Dr. Armerding's advice and privately pray over Romans 12:1-2? Write down your experience.
- Pray through the questions of Appendix 5.

Made in the USA
Lexington, KY
11 May 2013